D1517818

DOUG HICKS

NEARLY FORGOTTEN

The Amazing Story of the Glenn Pool,
Oklahoma's First World-Class Oil Field

For Shirley

TABLE OF CONTENTS

PROLOGUE

No other person has provided greater economic, social and cultural influence on Oklahoma *with a single act* and subsequently become less well-remembered than Bob Galbreath, the wildcatter who discovered the Glenn Pool a century ago.

The first major oil field in Oklahoma, the Glenn Pool yielded crude in a never-seen-before combination of great quantity and high quality, attracting the people, the money, the infrastructure and the national spotlight that made possible the rapid development of a powerful oil industry in a new state.

It all began with these words at 5 a.m. on November 22, 1905:

"Oil! Oil! My God, Bob, we got an oil well!"

Nothing has been quite the same since.

This book's mission:

Give both the man and the oil field their due, complete with the remarkable victories, failures, strengths and frailties that make up their uniquely American story.

Doug Hicks
September 2005

GLENN OIL FIELD
KIEFER. OK.

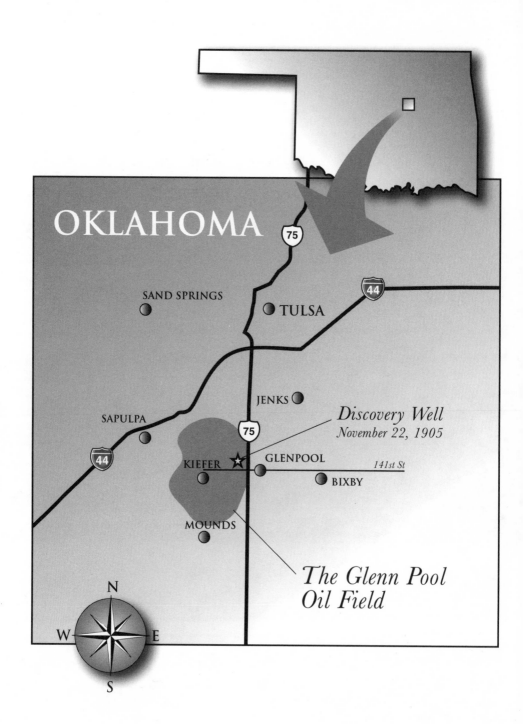

OKLAHOMA

SAND SPRINGS

TULSA

75

44

JENKS

SAPULPA

75

44

KIEFER

GLENPOOL

Discovery Well
November 22, 1905

141st St

BIXBY

MOUNDS

The Glenn Pool
Oil Field

N
W   E
S

Now and Then

In Search of the Ida Glenn

Heavy, white cumulus clouds glide across the Oklahoma sky as a mud-splattered pickup makes its way along meandering, graveled paths through sparsely treed, rolling pastures. The truck's diesel engine beats out a steady rhythm, mixing with the chka-chka-chka of a pump jack or the whine of a submersible pump at each stop.

For independent producer Eddie Rongey, it's another day in the oil field as he attends to 100 stripper wells pumping 300 barrels of crude oil from the Bartlesville sand. Each of the wells is producing from a single barrel to 12 barrels a day. Elsewhere in this same oil field, more than 250 other wells also are faithfully, seemingly timelessly, producing under the watchful eyes of other "independents."

The oil field is one of 3,100 in Oklahoma. Two thousand are still bringing raw energy from the ground. But Rongey isn't working just *any* oil field.

This is the Glenn Pool.

The Glenn Pool wasn't Oklahoma's first oil discovery – at least 19 others had come before it. But it was the best. For a glorious, frantic, bountiful, often wasteful time, it was unquestionably the greatest oil field in America, arguably the greatest in the world.

The never-seen-before combination of tremendous quantity and top quality crude oil made it unique. Discovered in 1905, the first major oil field in Oklahoma would build a multitude of oil-related companies, rescue one or two big ones, create fortunes, cause havoc and joy, and trigger widespread growth as a new industry materialized.

Oklahoma had never seen anything quite like it.

Honesty and corruption, generosity and greed, trust and distrust, wealth and poverty, good times and bad – all would arrive, reside, grow and emerge from the Glenn Pool.

Far beyond the borders of the forty-sixth state, the field would influence the nation's transformation from the industrial age to the energy age. Everything would change with oil – how the United States and the British powered their ships in the first world war; how innumerable products would be manufactured; how crops were harvested; how homes were heated; and, significantly, how John and Mary Public got from home to work and over to Aunt Minnie's on the weekend.

The field, situated in Creek and Tulsa counties, has been virtually given up for dead several times since its halcyon years in the early twentieth century. Each time, reports of its pending demise were premature. During the 1930s, as the bottom fell out of crude oil prices – and everything else – the Glenn Pool was all but abandoned.

Eddie Rongey has heard many of the hard-times stories of the Glenn Pool. The 40-year-old is third-generation, bib-overalls oilman. He was born a mile east of Kiefer, the heart of the field, "and never got away." By 17, he dropped out of school and was working in the oil patch. With a recent graduate-equivalency diploma in hand, he now serves on the Kiefer School Board and advises youngsters to stay in school.

His father, Ira, was born in a tiny work house in the field. Ira's father, Ollie, worked in a natural gasoline plant, stripping valuable liquids from the natural gas produced in the field. As a barefoot boy growing up in the Great Depression, Ira learned first-hand how good times can turn to bad when he walked alongside his father to the little grocery store at Sabo, one of dozens of towns that would vanish in Oklahoma during the bust side of the boom. The grocer told Ollie that he no longer could keep him "on the ticket" because all the workers at the gasoline plant had been laid off.

The news – true, as it turned out – was serious stuff in a time when no one drew, or imagined receiving, unemployment bucks from big-mother government. Towns dwindled or disappeared altogether in the down times. Jobless men and women "made do" any way they could – lard sandwiches, watery coffee, worn-out shoes, their soles stuffed with paper.

At the Tulsa Chamber of Commerce's fiftieth anniversary celebration of the Glenn Pool discovery, an optimistic speaker claimed that the venerable field would be good "for at least another

15 to 20 years." The seemingly fanciful forecast brought a smile to an oldtimer at the luncheon, Roy Dodd, a driller on the discovery well, the Ida Glenn No. 1.

The once legendary but later largely forgotten Glenn Pool is among the elite of Oklahoma's 26 oil fields that have achieved nationally recognized major status. At the time of the celebration in 1955, the Glenn Pool had produced 250 million barrels of oil. Today, the figure is well past the 330-million-barrel mark.

The Glenn Pool hit its stride in 1907, the year of Oklahoma statehood. By the end of the tumultuous year, it had already recorded a total of more than 27 million barrels of crude oil production. More than a few "tankies," scarred, tough-as-nails men, collapsed from the heat of that aught-seven summer in the all-out rush to build storage tanks as great amounts of oil were flowed into earthen pits. The field surpassed the 100-million-barrel mark during 1912, establishing it as one of the nation's major oil fields for all time.

Only five Oklahoma fields have produced 500 million barrels or more. The great Cushing Field, discovered in 1912 and the first field to eclipse the Glenn Pool, is among those five. The Cushing discovery was led and precipitated by the Glenn Pool boom, which attracted big money and interest in a westward movement in dreams of similar strikes – dreams that often came true.

The Glenn Pool has been successfully redrilled several times. The field's formation has been injected with steam and natural gas, and, predominantly, flooded with water in efforts to coax more of her treasure to the surface. The last significant drilling program ended in 1986.

"I really think someday, when the world is really hurting

for oil, the field will be redrilled again," says Eddie Rongey. Others also think the Glenn Pool will give birth to at least one more drilling program. The independent producers aren't holding their breaths for that to happen, but their hopes recently have been buoyed and their pocketbooks thickened by the dramatic upturn in crude oil prices.

"All the majors (large oil companies) are gone. Independents started the field, and independents are finishing it," Eddie says with pride and a hint to past, deep conflicts between the "bigs" and "littles" involved in the Glenn Pool long, long ago.

At a patch of handsome new homes at the eastern edge of Kiefer, he points to a fresh, wooden-fenced enclosure. "There's one of the original wells – still producing."

No one would have believed that possible a half- or a whole century ago. But the Glenn Pool has surprised, delighted and frustrated generations.

"If anyone tells you they know everything there is to be known about these wells or this field, they are really stupid or they're lying," the oilman says.

Tom Matson, an 87-year-old geologist, independent oilman and student of the Glenn Pool, agrees. He and former Tulsa mayors Bob LaFortune and Jim Hewgley together have been involved in the field since the early 1960s.

"One of the best wells we've got was drilled in 1907, and it's still producing. Those old wells just went on and on and on," Matson says.

People such as Matson and the Rongeys, who understand and appreciate the field, are few and growing fewer with each passing year. Currently, there is precious little to remind or inform anyone of the time that was.

At Glenpool, a Tulsa bedroom community named for the field, two markers rest behind a pair of blue trash barrels at the edge of U.S. 75. One of the markers proclaims, *Glenn Pool, World's Great Oil Pool*; the other, *First Gas Processing Plant West of the Mississippi River.* In the white-faced city hall building, an oil painting of an old-time oil field resides on the second floor. In nearby Black Gold Park, a rust-stained, wedge-shaped stone rests at the foot of a steel, toy-like derrick enclosed by a chain-link fence. Faded black lettering on the stone reads, *Ida Glenn Well No. 1.*

Visitors may think this is the home of the discovery well – but it isn't. The stone marker was moved from the actual well site many years ago. But where is the Ida Glenn?

Finding the well involves a bit of detective work and stumbling onto the right folks. Sam Shanks, a retired pipefitter, offers general directions to the well. He then provides the phone number of his brother, Alva Shanks, also a retired pipefitter.

Alva's home is nestled on a pretty, manicured plateau northwest of Glenpool's downtown business district. Quiet-spoken and amiable, he relates that Bob and Ida Glenn once lived over yonder, at the far end of his sprawling front yard. The discovery well came in on the 160-acre federal allotment of Ida Glenn, a one-eighth-blood Creek Indian whose Alabama-based ancestors were force-marched in the 1830s into Indian Territory, a part of what would become Oklahoma.

Shanks walks through the yard to the edge of a heavily treed area and points to a grave, the final resting place of the Glenns' 2-year-old son, Elmer. At the bottom of the weathered gravestone, barely legible, are the words, *budded on earth to bloom in heaven.*

He says the Glenn home, one of about 12 in the area when the oil was discovered, once rested on his 10-acre tract of the original allotment. His directions to the Ida Glenn No. 1 lead to a bend in a mobile home park, below his land, and across a wet-weather creek. Vine-laden, skinny trees poke into the overcast sky. A small-diameter pipe, nearly rusted in two, spans the creek bed.

Shanks had warned that nothing would be found at the discovery well site. He was right. There is nothing there. What occurred in those wee morning hours a century ago has been physically lost to time, man and nature. The well's shaft was plugged with concrete more than 40 years ago; the stone marker lugged to the Black Gold Park after a pipeline was built through the woods.

The lack of anything at the discovery well site, supposedly hallowed ground for keepers of Oklahoma's rich oil history, is eerie. The anonymity of the well, however, is largely in keeping with how little is known, remembered or commemorated regarding the wildcatter who made it all happen – Bob Galbreath.

His name appears on no buildings, museums or large monuments. It also is absent from the rolls of numerous oilmen honored by the Oklahoma industry he fired up and led for a relatively brief time.

It was here on this unmarked spot of land that the 6-foot-2 native Ohioan with a fourth-grade education got some shut-eye a few paces from the noisy drilling rig, its coal-fired steam engine sending up gasps of smelly soot into the chilly night air.

Pushing age 42, he was vibrant and sparkle-eyed but no longer young in a time when the average life span was 54 years. He already had lived several lifetimes of adventure, including the great land runs into Oklahoma, town marshal and deputy United States marshal, federal commissioner, Pony Express rider, postmaster, seller of dreams, and beer-drinker with the Apache warrior Geronimo.

At the turn of the century, Galbreath had been attracted to Red Fork, situated a few miles southwest of Tulsa, to see his first oil well. He was so fascinated by the sight that he tried his hand at finding the stuff, with modest success. Discovered in 1901, the Red Fork Field never lived up to its ballyhooed beginnings, but it sent Galbreath on the trail of the fabulous Glenn Pool.

At 5 a.m. on November 22, 1905, Galbreath's life and life in Oklahoma would change with the sight, smell, sound and feel of a lot of oil – good oil. The changes occurred slowly at first, then with alarming speed.

In some ways, Galbreath would mimic the historic Glenn Pool. Like her, he would rise to glory and fade, but never really disappear. Made rich by his find, he would not keep his wealth. For a shining moment, he was regaled as the *King of the Wildcatters*. That, too, would be lost. He would try to make lightning strike twice, try to find another truly magnificent Glenn Pool. There would not be another one – not for him. A staunch Democrat, he played in local and national politics, ran unsuccessfully for mayor of Tulsa, and in his later years churned out lengthy, typewritten letters to friends, newspaper editors and fellow Democrats, usually with advice on the industry he loved and the big-oil and big-business corporations he despised.

This is the story of the Glenn Pool, Bob Galbreath – the uncommon common man – and a sampling of the great field's characters and kind hearts.

ADVENTURER, LAWMAN, WILDCATTER

BOB GALBREATH

he oxen churned up clumps of rich, black soil as they and the huge log behind them accumulated speed down the long hill leading to the Ohio farming community's water-powered mill. Perched atop a sack of corn straddling the log, young Bob Galbreath prodded the bovines in the rumps with a stick to increase their pace.

People gathered to see if the tall, brown-eyed boy would make it down to the bottom in one piece. A cheer rose as he did. Now, the corn would be ground into meal for his mother, Sarah, and the log sawed into lumber for his father, Robert.

In the 1870s, boys like Galbreath created their own fun, games and adventures. This one taught him balance, which he would later draw on as he deftly guided thoroughbreds in hotly contested harness races. The youngster came by his love for fast and good horses honestly; his family had been involved in blooded horses for generations before Bob's birth on December 22, 1863. Twenty-two would be his lucky number for life.

The Galbreath farm was near Darbyville, but the community was known locally by another name – Frogeye – for the countless frogs that inhabited a swamp, where they croaked out melodies at day's end.

As evening came, glass-chimneyed lamps fueled by a new, cleaner-burning illuminant called kerosene pushed back the darkness in the Galbreaths' log home. In 1855, a moonlighting Yale chemistry professor had developed the process for refining kerosene from "rock oil." Four years later, an off-work railroad conductor, Edwin Drake, with the made-up title of "Colonel," brought in the first commercially successful oil well in the United States at Titusville, Pennsylvania. These two events created an industry centered on kerosene for lamps and lubricants for the growing number of machines doing the labor of man and animals. One man, John D. Rockefeller, and one company, Standard Oil, operating under a plethora of different names, would come to dominate the emerging industry.

Certainly, none of this was of any concern to Bob Galbreath the boy. But critically timed events in the embryonic oil industry eventually would capture his attention and lead him to discover what was, for years, the greatest oil field in the nation. As for Rockefeller and Standard Oil, they would be a never-healing sore, and reason enough to rail against big-oil, big-business and any person or political party that appeared to support them.

Galbreath would become the staunchest of Democrats.

For now, in Pickaway County, Ohio, he was content. He had quit school and was working on the farm – commonplace in 1870s America. Four years of schooling had taught him to read, write and cipher as well as most, better than many. He was well read for the times and kept up on current events, a habit he would continue throughout his unusually long lifetime.

By age 20, the young man had read and heard of land – for the taking – in Oklahoma, considered to be among the final frontiers of the country. It was enough to send him on his way to southwestern Kansas in the summer of 1884, nearly five years before the Oklahoma District would be legally opened by presidential proclamation. By that fall, Galbreath thought better of his hopes and plans to homestead 160 acres in Oklahoma. Besides the fact that he couldn't do it legally, he figured that building a place up just to be rousted off it by the U.S. Cavalry wasn't smart thinking. He returned home to Ohio, where he spent the better part of four years successfully harness racing. By the end of his racing stint, he was driving for one of the best stables in the country.

Galbreath, still on the farm.

WANDERLUST TRUMPS STEADINESS

Galbreath loved adventure, trying something – anything – new. As an inherent part of that trait, wanderlust trumped steadiness. In 1888, he left Ohio again and joined up with younger brother Charlie in California. There, the two worked at this odd job and that. Bob was down to his last five dollars when they agreed to return to family and familiarity. They "invested" their last few dollars with a jobless pal who was good at faro, a card game in which money is waged on the top card of the dealer's deck.

Quickly, the brothers had more than enough to buy rail tickets home. Trouble was, their friend didn't want to quit playing. Years later, Bob would recall that it was "a tossup" whether he and Charlie would take their winnings or get shot trying. In January of 1889, they boarded a train that would carry them to Texas and up to the town of Eufaula, in Indian Territory. There, Bob became visibly excited as he read that President Benjamin Harrison had proclaimed that the Oklahoma District, also known as the Unassigned Lands, would be opened to homesteaders on April 22.

Twenty-two. Galbreath's birth date. *Surely,* he thought, *this is fate. This is meant to be.*

During the next few months back home, Galbreath was like a child waiting for Christmas – in April. At high noon on the day after Easter Sunday, he and another brother, Herman, joined tens of thousands in the 1889 Land Run, the first and most famous of them all.

To this day, no one really knows how many homesteaders – on horses and mules, in wagons and buggies, inside and atop railroad coaches and cattle cars, on bicycles and on foot – turned out that day. Fifty-thousand is a middle-ground guesstimate. Somewhere in that number of "Boomers" were Lon Chaney, who would become famous as a silent-motion-picture star, and William Wrigley, of chewing gum note.

A 16-year-old Irish girl – small, pretty and headstrong – also was among the sea of people.

Some started the great race at Purcell. Others rushed in from the eastern and western borders. Riding horses bred for long distances, the Galbreaths – and the largest single part of the crazy crowd – began from the south end of the 60-mile deep Cherokee Strip. They had been told to pay no mind to the Indians, who had been informed that this invasion through their land was only temporary. Only four years later, the Strip would be opened to settlement.

An 89er family near Guthrie. Notice the home improvement: rough-hewn logs fronting the dugout.

Not long after the start, it was clear to the Galbreath brothers that some hadn't played by the rules. "Sooners" rose up from a myriad of hiding places to stake their claims before the "Boomers." It also became clear that not everyone was going to get a piece of the "promised land," even though it encompassed almost two million acres in what would become six counties.

Many left poorer than they arrived, if that were possible; others didn't have money or food enough to leave and sought work in the instant towns. Guthrie, among them, went from nothing to a population of 10,000 by sunset. It would become the territorial capital and state capital. Bob Galbreath would have a sideline role in the infamous theft of the Great Seal of Oklahoma, which was stolen in 1910 and whisked away to the new capital, Oklahoma City.

Bob and Herman drove wooden stakes into the four corners of their 160-acre piece of land before the sun set on the day of the run. Bright and early the next day, they began chopping down trees for their new home. This was the brothers' new beginning, the place where they would live, farm, propagate and prosper.

The morning outlasted the dream. Barely visible at first, a battered wagon appeared on the sunlit horizon. The sounds of crying children sheltered inside mingled with the sight of their stoic-faced parents perched on the buckboard. They had been too slow to stake a claim. The brothers warmly greeted them and shared a mess of flapjacks. Over cups of black coffee, they handed their dream to the landless family for no more than the ten-dollar cost of filing a claim at a U.S. Land Office. They also gave them most of their food, which had arrived with a trailing supply wagon.

This kind of generosity would be repeated many times by

the older Galbreath. He felt pretty good about what he'd just done. Besides, the rules required homesteaders to live full-time on the land for five years before it was theirs. Bob wasn't nearly ready to stay in one place that long. With nary a look back or a regret – a characteristic he would reflect in the personal ups and downs of the Glenn Pool oil boom – he and his brother headed southeast to Edmond and fresh adventures.

There, Bob bought dwellings and tracts from those who had lost their passion and sold them to homeless newcomers who wanted to stay. He soon found himself comfortably strapping on his .44 caliber "hawgleg" revolver, so named because of its long barrel and plow-handle grip, as the town marshal and later as a deputy U.S. marshal for the area.

The hawgleg was never out of easy reach – except for that one time. Wearing a heavy, long coat buttoned all the way up to keep out the winter wind, Galbreath strode into a grocery store and locked eyes with a man who looked vaguely familiar. In a flash, he linked the face to a wanted poster, realized he couldn't get to his single-action revolver, walked briskly across the wooden floor, stuck his hand in the coat's right pocket, and pushed at the man's belly. The heavy plug of tobacco in the lawman's pocket must have felt enough like a gun; the outlaw threw up his hands upon Galbreath's command, "Don't move. Don't move. You're under arrest."

For most people, one great land run would be adventure enough for a lifetime. Galbreath would be involved in a total of four from 1889 to 1893. He showed up just to soak in the excitement of one, and served as an official in another.

"DO YOU KETCH ME?"

Always looking for adventures as much or more than opportunities, Galbreath inked a Wells Fargo contract to run mail and goods from Edmond some 60 miles through a sprinkling of towns leading to the Sac and Fox Indian Agency office in what would become Lincoln County. The land was familiar – Bob had made the September 1891 Land Run into the "surplus" lands of the Sac and Fox, Iowa and Potawatomi on his lucky-number date, twenty-two.

Along the route, made alternately by horseback and wagon, homesteaders cooked for him as they read fresh mail from loved ones hundreds of miles away. Roads were built, with Galbreath and the homesteaders often sharing in the work.

When not driving a wagon, Galbreath relied on three fresh horses each way. The Pony Express rider would recall decades later that eight horses gave up the ghost in a single year of keeping that Star Route alive. On one memorable run, he outran a tornado, only to arrive in the next town and sadly realize that it had been flattened by another twister. Duties of the job ranged from outwitting outlaws as he transported saddlebags of money to delivering costume jewelry and love potions. It seems that many of the homesteaders had sent in coupons from cans of coffee in exchange for the trinkets and the dubiously promising elixir.

He also tried a stint as postmaster of Edmond, but that job had way too much "stay-put" to it. Bob Galbreath clearly had itchy feet, only partly assuaged by his marriage in 1892 to Mary Ellen Kivlehan – that pretty Irish girl in the '89 Land Run whose parents had settled in Edmond.

A member of the first graduating class of the Territorial

Normal College of Edmond, Mary Ellen had gone against her father's wishes by marrying the lawman, who during the courtship was prone to fire rounds from his long-snouted revolver as he rode by the Kivlehan home. The father threatened to bring out his shotgun if the rambunctious man, nine years older than his daughter, didn't pull in his reins.

Galbreath's wife would spend her lifetime trying to get him to quit ending his talks with, "Do you ketch me?" – words he had used since an Ohio farm boy. She eventually realized, with more amusement than irritation, that her minor but continued effort toward his refinement had failed. They raised four children, a girl, Leona, and three boys, Robert, Frank and Glenn Pool.

Mary Ellen Galbreath put out a couple of newspapers, first in Edmond and then in Perry, where more of the Ohio Galbreath clan settled when the Cherokee Strip was opened. At Perry, in 1893, Galbreath met and became friends with Charlie Colcord, who staked his claim on the very spot where he had been accidentally knocked down from his horse. It turned out to be the best business lot in Perry.

Colcord was lucky that way. He would become a wealthy Oklahoma City oilman and civic leader. Honors and tributes flowed to Colcord. By 1929, five years before his death, he would be inducted into the Oklahoma Hall of Fame. No such high honor would come to his friend Galbreath.

Galbreath would move, again, in 1896 to Shawnee, where he would serve for the better part of three years as a U.S. Commissioner, whose duties included serving as a judge, determining who would go free and who would face trial in Oklahoma Territory.

What had made him feel safe, the ever-ready revolver, would forever disappear from his bedside following a frightening night in the Galbreath home. Mary Ellen had arisen from bed to check on the children while Bob slept. Long after the incident, he told his son Frank what happened next.

"Her soft, 'Are you awake, Bob?' came at the same second I reached for my pistol on the night stand, cocked it, and started to blast the silhouette in the doorway. I hadn't realized until then that your mother was not at my side. I shook all that night just like I had the ague (a sharp fever), and I never had another gun in the bedroom, and I never will."

A shotgun for keeping nosey folks away from a successful wildcat well? That would be an entirely different matter for a different time.

While Galbreath was in Shawnee, a wildcat well named for a 6-year-old child, Nellie Johnstone, came in on a bank of the Caney River near Bartlesville. Discovered on April 15, 1897, it would become well-known as Oklahoma's first commercially successful oil well but wouldn't be brought into full production until 1903, when rail transport, and later a pipeline, to a Standard Oil refinery in Kansas was provided.

BEERS FOR GERONIMO

In 1899, Galbreath shuffled northwest to Oklahoma City, set up a real estate office at Third and Broadway, and within days partnered up with the lucky fellow who had been knocked off his horse in Perry six years earlier. By all accounts, the business of Colcord and Galbreath prospered. Galbreath's job was little different from what he had done off and on since arriving in Edmond a decade earlier; he was selling more new dreams.

Ever drawn to a good horse race, the former deputy marshal found himself serving as caretaker to Geronimo, the aging Apache medicine man, warrior and acclaimed chieftain, held in what amounted to the world's largest house arrest at Fort Sill. Transported as a drawing card to the Oklahoma City fairgrounds track, Geronimo had but one request – beer – before he would mount up to race against a former Indian scout.

Galbreath struck a deal: one beer after the race, two if Geronimo won. The old warrior collected his two beers.

Among those who turned out to see Geronimo that day in Oklahoma City were two youngsters, Dave and Miller Williams, who had traveled by horseback from Purcell. The Glenn Pool and the other oil discoveries that followed would prompt the brothers to move their business from Fort Smith, Arkansas, to Tulsa in 1916. Williams Brothers, known today simply as Williams, became the premier pipeline builder in the world. It would be one of literally thousands of businesses attracted to the *Oil Capital of the World.*

Judging from his past restlessness, it was unlikely that Galbreath would sell Oklahoma City real estate for long. In the very early part of the twentieth century, events were bubbling to the surface; some would twist and turn not only the oil industry, but Galbreath himself.

Thomas Edison, back in 1879, had publicly demonstrated a practical electric light bulb, which was finally taking hold in larger cities and would eventually extinguish the countless kerosene-fueled lamps across America. That appeared to be bad news for the oil industry. But the four-stroke, internal-combustion engine was coming into its own. These engines – in automobiles, airplanes, ships, tractors, and countless industrial applications – would use fuel refined from oil, far outstripping previous demand for kerosene. Also, there was a guy named Henry Ford, born the same year as Bob Galbreath, who wanted to get away from his engineering job at Edison Electric and build his own automobile – one for the masses, not the wealthy. It sounded like a wacky idea.

The impact in Oklahoma from those events in the very early 1900s was subtle, at best. What wasn't subtle at all was Spindletop, an oil well drilled on a salt dome a few miles south of Beaumont, a Texas town of 9,000 near the Gulf of Mexico.

Spindletop's Long Reach

On January 10, 1901, mud lapped up on the rotary drilling table atop the salt dome. The brown, gooey stuff shot up the derrick. The drilling crew ran. Six tons of pipe belched completely out of the hole and into the Texas sky. Dismay set in. Moments later, gas blew out. Something heavy and dark green followed way past the derrick's crown block – oil! Some would describe it as the "discovery that changed the world." Certainly, the well and the prolific field that swiftly grew there drew nationwide attention.

Spindletop made every would-be wildcatter want to strike it rich somewhere, anywhere. So, when the Sue A. Bland No. 1 well came in at Red Fork, a community a few miles southwest of Tulsa, on June 24 – five months after Spindletop – the shallow discovery well garnered far more attention than merited.

The *Kansas City Times,* the *Tulsa Democrat,* forerunner to *The Tulsa Tribune,* and the *Muskogee Weekly Phoenix* all shouted the news.

Word-of-mouth soon had it that the site just might outdo Spindletop. And the little farm and cattle town quickly became a boomtown, with a makeshift eatery set up right at the well.

In Oklahoma City, a car was added to the train to accommodate extra passengers lining up for trips to Tulsa and on to the well. Aboard that special car on June 28 were Bob Galbreath, his real-estate partner Charlie Colcord and C. G. "Gristmill" Jones, a railroad builder. More than 5,000 people had converged at Red Fork by the time they arrived.

Galbreath would claim that it was the first oil well he had ever seen.

For decades, it would be argued who should be given due credit for the well – experienced oilmen Jesse Heydrick and J. S. Wick or local physicians Fred Clinton and C. W. Bland, husband of Creek Indian Sue Bland, on whose property the well had been spudded. People rushing to the site during the boom couldn't have cared less.

The Red Fork Field would not "outdo" Spindletop, not even come close. Red Fork was not a great producer. But it drew oilmen and speculators by the thousands to the area, caused Tulsa investors to build a vital bridge across the Arkansas River, and set

Spindletop, near Beaumont, Texas, created a fervor to find oil and was the main reason the Red Fork Field drew more attention than it deserved.

off a wave of band-playing, chest-pounding town boosters across the nation. All of this helped the little town of Tulsa grow rapidly, much to the chagrin of rivals such as Sapulpa. Most important, the commotion at Red Fork placed Galbreath in range of the future Glenn Pool.

Noted historian Dr. Kenny Franks, author of numerous books including *The Rush Begins*, wrote that skullduggery was used to attract investors – such as Galbreath, Colcord and Jones – to Red Fork:

To encourage potential investors, and thereby provide additional funds for continued drilling, (the Sue A. Bland No. 1 parties) devised a method to keep up the public interest. It bordered on outright deceit. By placing a canvas bag over the well's bailer, and then lowering the contraption to the bottom of the well, they were able to hold the escaping oil and gas in check. After enough pressure had built up to throw the crude high into the air, the bailer and canvas bag were hurriedly drawn up the hole. With the blockage removed, the crude, pushed by the gas pressure, rushed up the pipe and was thrown as high as 10 feet into the air.

As a result of such theatrics, several oilmen began additional wells in the Red Fork area in spite of the question of unresolved legal titles. Their efforts received a boost when the federal government sold the townsite lots of Red Fork at auction in the spring of 1901. One of the first developers was Galbreath.

The Sue Bland No. 1 discovery well opened the Red Fork Field in 1901.

22

RAILING AGAINST STANDARD OIL

A dizzying array of federal rules and regulations had clouded, thwarted and stalled oil exploration in Indian Territory for many years. It came down to whether American Indians, who had been resettled in Indian Territory in the nineteenth century, could lease the rights to the valuable oil and gas beneath their feet. In the end, they could, but federal bureaucracy, confusion and delays were part and parcel of drilling for oil in Indian Territory.

Backed by Colcord and Jones, Galbreath quickly began drilling for oil in Red Fork – before legally obtaining a lease. He reportedly managed to stay out of jail only through his influence and friendship with Creek Indian Chief Pleasant Porter. The chief's sister was the wife of John Yargee, on whose farm Galbreath was busily drilling.

(In 1949, a newspaper reported that Galbreath had taken his lease-rights case all the way to Washington, where Secretary of the Interior Ethan Hitchcock turned him down. "But Galbreath then obtained an audience with President Theodore Roosevelt, who saw to it that the Yargee lease was approved." It's worth noting that Galbreath in his senior years was known to embellish his stories. So it is likely that, as time passed, the story of Galbreath's near-jail experience grew.)

Despite a fire that destroyed his first rig and torrential rains that slowed his initial progress, Galbreath had some success at Red Fork. He also got his first taste – a bitter taste – of Standard Oil. Operating under the name of Prairie Oil and Gas, Standard controlled and set the price for most of the oil in Kansas. Red Fork production flowed inside a Prairie pipeline to its refinery at

Neodesha, Kansas. Galbreath's joy at bringing in a 125-barrel-a-day well northeast of Red Fork turned to bitter resentment after Prairie sent field agents to view the producer. As an immediate result of that visit, according to Galbreath, the price of Red Fork oil fell from 85 cents a barrel to 50 cents. And most of that was consumed by transportation charges to the refinery.

John D. Rockefeller, the founder of Standard, once said that "God gave me my money." Galbreath figured that God didn't give the frail, ruthless genius the right to take his. Late in life, the wildcatter would relate that he had gladly spent "a million dollars" fighting the huge, octopus-like company. Ultimately, the Standard empire would be dismantled through the efforts of a spinster journalist, Ida Tarbell; a United States president; federal courts; and the Supreme Court – but too late to help Galbreath.

At least one of the decisions made by Galbreath and his backers would seem, with a century of hindsight, just plain bone-headed. Many of the Red Fork wells produced not oil but gas. They considered piping the less-valuable stuff over to Tulsa, thought better of it, and then sold their Red Fork interests to Glenn Braden. He and three others would establish Oklahoma Natural Gas. That company, now a division of **ONEOK**, serves some 820,000 customers in the Sooner state.

Within a few years, the Red Fork oil enterprise was down on its heels. So, too, was Galbreath. But wildcatters are gamblers by nature, and this one had an ace up his sleeve.

In his first summer at Red Fork, Galbreath had driven a buggy 10 or 12 miles south to have a look-around. He was fascinated by the mounds that rose up from the rolling prairie, probably because Spindletop, the Texas oil field, was drilled on what came to be called Big Hill.

He camped the night of July 3, 1901, on Eck Brock's 320-acre farm. On Independence Day, Galbreath roamed north onto the 160-acre farm of Bob and Ida Glenn. Ida Estelle Berryhill Glenn was a one-eighth-blood Creek Indian. The land amounted to a federal payment of sorts for the anguish, tears and deaths her ancestors suffered while being force-marched from Alabama to Indian Territory in the 1830s. Among the original group of 630 attempting the migration, 161 perished.

Bob Glenn wanted to show Galbreath something – a limestone ledge not far from the simple farmhouse. The rock, which contained dark stains, had been quarried to build houses. Galbreath broke off a chunk of the soft limestone. His dark eyes widened and his thick mustache quivered as he peered at a globule of oil.

Galbreath told Glenn to keep quiet about this. Glenn replied that all his neighbors – there were about 12 homes scattered in an area that locals called the Glenn – already knew about it. He said the darned stuff also was on some of his neighbors' places and occasionally formed a black sheen on the creeks. Galbreath took a deep breath and, as calmly as possible, told Glenn to not tell another soul.

Ida fixed dinner. After the meal, Bob Glenn and Galbreath talked some more and shook hands. He would lease their land and drill for oil there once the lease was federally approved. Galbreath returned more than two and one-half years later with a couple of small-time investors. In exchange for $45 – less than 30 cents an acre – and a one-eighth interest in all production, the Glenns gave Galbreath the right to drill on their property. But his small-time investors became smaller still, disappearing altogether.

Hijacking Some Help

As time passed, Galbreath was at the end of his wits trying to get the Glenn lease approved while also trying to find someone to fund the drilling. The Red Fork Field, in his words, was "practically abandoned."

"My various partners ran hot, then cold, on the idea of the well down in the mounds country," he said. "Even Roy Dodd, my partner in the drilling contracting business at Red Fork, took a dim view of the deal.

"I was pumping two little wells at Red Fork belonging to Frank Chesley," Galbreath said. "As he well knew, I was making about enough to break even on the deal."

Chesley had a checkered past. He was, according to author and historian Bob Gregory, *a lady killer whom love had made a refugee. He'd come to the territories on the lam, got mixed up in the land runs, helped found the village of Keystone (west of Tulsa), and was believed connected with a group shipping alcoholic patent medicine into Indian Territory.*

Galbreath would described Chesley as a "restless devil" with a lot of energy and an outgoing, likeable personality. In his senior years, he would fondly remember Chesley as the "best field man I ever knew" and "a good ol' boy." The description, however, revealed more about Galbreath than it did Chesley, for their friendship would prove very costly to the wildcatter.

On this particular day, Chesley had dropped by to make sure his two little wells were still being pumped. Galbreath saw it as an opportunity to hijack him then and there.

He told his friend a little white lie – the power was off and the wells were shut down. Then he said, "Frank, it's a nice day for a buckboard ride to the Glenn area, where I'll show you the best drilling location in all creation."

"Hell, Bob, I need those two barrels production from these wells just to keep eating regular."

"Boy, are you in trouble and headed for a long, lean, hungry spell, 'cause till you do me the courtesy of looking at the country down there, I'm not going to pump your damn wells," Galbreath replied.

Shoved onto the buckboard, Chesley told Galbreath that anyone who extorted and hijacked wasn't much of a friend. At the Glenn farm, Galbreath led Chesley to the limestone ledge, broke off a little chunk, and, sure enough, another pearl of oil seeped from the stone.

According to Galbreath, Chesley almost "wet his pants."

By the wildcatter's own account given decades after the fact, gaining government approval of the Glenn lease took "four long years" from the time he first met Bob and Ida in the summer of 1901 to when he was notified that he could actually drill on their farm. (Other published accounts reported that the Glenn lease was approved much earlier, on September 22 – Galbreath's lucky number – in 1904.)

With the lease in hand, Galbreath finally managed to round up his crew. Roy Dodd agreed to provide the use of his rig if Galbreath would pay him five bucks a day as the driller. Shorty Miller, also an excellent driller, was hired to oversee the underfinanced little venture. And Frank Chesley – well, he was still excited from seeing the oil hidden in the limestone.

In addition to Dodd's rig, a motley collection of equipment, some of it described as junk, was begged, borrowed and lugged from the Red Fork Field.

Bringing in the Ida Glenn

In early fall of 1905, Galbreath, Chesley, Dodd and Miller began drilling not far from the Glenns' farmhouse. Compared to the rotary rig used at Spindletop, Dodd's cable-tool rig, also known as a "standard," was unsophisticated. Spindletop lost more money in pipe when it exploded out of the hole than Dodd's entire rig cost. A rotary rig *drills* the bit into the earth; a standard rig *pounds* it in. From the drill floor, Miller and Dodd continually rotated the bit to provide a fresh bite with each downward thrust of the heavy tools.

Using coal-fired, steam-boiler power, drillers Dodd and Miller picked up the tools – bit, stem and jars held by a Manila rope and heavy cable – and let 'er go. Again and again. The slack had to be just right, every time. Too much, and the hole would go crooked, might be ruined. Too little, and the bit wouldn't land with full force.

On what would become the discovery well, there was another little matter Dodd and Miller were concerned about. No casing was used to protect the hole from cave-ins or flooding. Galbreath couldn't afford to buy the pipe.

"They just kept pounding down," says independent producer Ira Rongey, born in the Glenn Pool at the onset of the Great Depression. "If it got too muddy, they'd pull the tools out and run a bailer down there. This went on day and night. They probably made five, maybe six feet in a run; then they'd start over again."

All four lived at the rig. As Dodd and Miller took turns drilling, Galbreath and Chesley kept the boiler stoked with coal. They slept in a shack. They ate simple meals, washed down with

15-cents-a-pound coffee to keep them awake.

In November, when they had reached a depth of 1,300 feet, Galbreath told onlookers that the project was being abandoned. It wasn't true, but he wanted to shoo them off just in case the well did come in. The fewer people who knew, the lower the price for gaining additional leases.

On the morning of November 22 – Galbreath's lucky number – operations were temporarily stopped at a depth of 1,448 feet.

"The hole was not making any water, so caving was not a problem, though the hole was wide open from top to bottom," Galbreath said. Although they already were past the point where they had hoped to strike oil – and they were broke – they chose to hammer on.

Galbreath, now replaced at the rig by Chesley, stretched out on a cot in the shack and quickly fell asleep. At 5 a.m., Chesley ran to the shack and pushed oil-stained sand, pulled up by the bailer, beneath Galbreath's long, broad nose.

"Oil! Oil!," Chesley shouted as he shoved Galbreath off

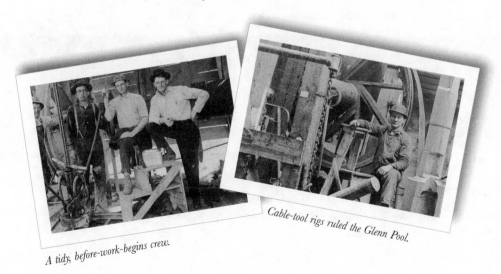

A tidy, before-work-begins crew.

Cable-tool rigs ruled the Glenn Pool.

the cot. "My God, Bob, we got an oil well!"

Galbreath reached the derrick floor "in about three jack-rabbit jumps." Oil spilled over the floor from the overturned bailer. Dodd calmly told Galbreath they were at 1,458 feet.

Oil began slopping onto the thick boards of the drill floor.

"As we watched in wonderment, it mounted from a quiet, gaseous stream into an increasingly forceful column of golden riches that rapidly mounted higher and higher and higher," Galbreath said. "Then all hell broke loose, and the Ida E. Glenn flowed mightily over the derrick top, over the crown block, high into the air above."

The well could be seen from the Glenn home. Inside, Ida Glenn exclaimed, "We're not going to be poor anymore."

She was right. Their life would be good, but they would not stay at "the Glenn."

The day after the discovery, the *Tulsa Democrat* reported that the well might be a 50-barrel producer or better. *No definite news is obtainable at this time, and it may be several days for information concerning it to come along – it being claimed that a rigid "quarantine" is being maintained, no one being allowed to get to the derrick.*

The *Mounds Enterprise* reported, *The well is heavily guarded, and no one is allowed to go near it. Just why this is done no one can explain. But it is thought that it's for the purpose of securing more leases.*

Indeed, people were being kept away from the discovery well by words of warning backed by the business end of a shotgun. It was a "tight hole" – goings-on were kept hush-hush – one of the first in Indian Territory, but not for long.

The Ida Glenn flowed at 85 barrels a day – a small amount when compared with wells that quickly followed, but a lot when there is no place to put it. Galbreath said they tried to shut it in, but it "just couldn't be did. We succeeded in controlling it down and running a little of the oil in some old tankage and into hastily dug earthen pits."

Broke, Galbreath turned to friend and former business associate Charlie Colcord, over at Oklahoma City, for $2,500. In turn, Concord received an interest in the Glenn lease. For this investment, he later would come away with $400,000.

The wildcatter also tapped John Mitchell, an attorney and future mayor of Tulsa, for $1,000. He tried in vain to cash the note in Tulsa, succeeded at Red Fork, and was asked by the banker why he hadn't come to him in the first place. "I didn't know you had a thousand dollars in this bank," Galbreath replied.

Galbreath, Chesley, Colcord and Mitchell formed the Creek Oil Company, one of hundreds that would pop up in the Glenn Pool.

With cash in hand, Galbreath could set loose Chesley, "the best field man" he ever knew, to buy leases. He gathered up about 600 acres in

The Ida Glenn No. 1.

all, nearly a square mile. The cash also allowed them to put protective pipe down the Ida Glenn. This wouldn't be accomplished, however, until February of 1906.

Selling Out

It is legend and myth that the Glenn Pool instantly boomed. Its initial growth was relatively mild, partly because the discovery well wasn't a particularly big producer. Also, Galbreath kept things as hush-hush as he could in the very early going. Additionally, there simply was no immediate way to transport the oil. A two-inch pipeline was built from the field to Red Fork and on to the Galbreath-dreaded Standard Oil tankage and refinery in Kansas. That little pipeline had the effect of sticking a straw in the ocean. Big money would flow into the field as much larger pipelines were built to it, linking up to refineries in deep Texas, as well as Kansas.

Galbreath drilled at least 69 successful wells in the Glenn Pool, with only one dry hole – on Eck Brock's land next to the Glenn farm. But elsewhere on the Brock land, he brought in one of the best producers in the entire field. He referred to the Eck Brock No. 3, which initially produced 5,000 barrels a day, as Old Glory. It was on the same spot he had camped the night before first meeting the Glenns on the Fourth of July in 1901. Likewise, his other efforts on the Glenn farm resulted in excellent producers, far exceeding the discovery well.

The Glenn Pool provided Galbreath with the potential to become a Harry Sinclair or a Bill Skelly, who built large, fully integrated oil companies from nothing. But he was neither a Sinclair nor a Skelly. He tried to build a refinery, but it never took off. He traveled to New York to discuss the possibility of building of a large-diameter pipeline to refineries on the Gulf Coast. A big newspaper story came out of the talks, but nothing else.

During 1907 and 1908, he bought out his various partners,

with the exception of his good friend Frank Chesley. A biographical sketch written on Galbreath in 1908 said, in part, that he had *become wealthy and one of the largest producers of oil in the country. It has been his policy never to sell an oil property that he develops so long as it will produce. Therefore, he is essentially a producer rather than a speculator.* (Sourced from an independent affiliate of the American History and Genealogy Project.)

Only one year later, in 1909, with the Glenn Pool still crazily booming, Galbreath sold out to J. Edgar Crosbie for $500,000 – nearly $10 million in today's dollars. Chesley had sold his interests to Crosbie the previous month for $250,000. (According to Galbreath's son Frank, the total amount paid to Galbreath was $700,000 – $500,000 from Crosbie and $200,000 from the Texas Company, or Texaco.)

By several reports, Galbreath had grown tired of running a company, especially by himself. He also grew weary of constantly fretting over erratic, often-declining oil prices controlled by much larger players in Kansas, Texas and points beyond.

He still had, he reasoned, Bald Hill. He and others had found oil on Captain Severs' ranch south of Haskell, Oklahoma, on November 22 – that lucky number again – 1907. He took some pride in the fact that it was the first wildcat after statehood. There was still work to be done down there in the Bald Hill Field. And, surely, there would be more fields to come, maybe even greater fields.

William Mellon understood men like Galbreath. William was the nephew of the enormously wealthy Pittsburgh-banking Mellon brothers who had funded Spindletop, marking the beginning of what came to be called Gulf Oil. The nephew is quoted in one of the best of the innumerable books written on oil, *The Prize,* by Daniel Yergin:

For a great many, the oil business was more like an epic card game, in which the excitement was worth more than great stacks of chips. None of us was disposed to stop, take his money out of the wells, and go home. Each well, whether successful or unsuccessful, provided the stimulus to drill another.

The nephew himself had such "oil fever," according to *The Prize*, but his uncles' guidance prevented him from falling victim to it.

Oilmen such as the Mellons, Sinclair, Skelly, J. Paul Getty, Frank Phillips and others were smart enough, and became rich enough, to integrate their businesses. It was that or become prey to Standard Oil. There were notable exceptions, such as independent oil producers and partners Robert McFarlin and James Chapman, who got their start in the Glenn Pool. But they were wise and prudent businessmen, smart enough to sell out at the right times. Frank Phillips' brother, Waite Phillips, also fit into that rarefied category.

THE LONG GOODBYE

Galbreath's departure from the Glenn Pool fit not only his nature but his life pattern. Excepting marriage, he simply wasn't "built" to stay at the same thing in the same place for long. He also happened to be generous and trusting – great-sounding traits, but they didn't always serve him well.

In 1910, he and Mary Ellen busied themselves overseeing construction of a $50,000, three-story mansion on South Boulder Avenue's *Golden Mile*, so-called for the row of oil millionaires' palaces. Fancy, high-priced and high-powered cars sped down the street into the night, their drivers often "deep in their cups," as described by a *Tulsa World* reporter.

Fortunately, Galbreath had tucked away enough memories for a long lifetime. He loved to retell how he put one over on Standard Oil by leaving his rig up after his lone dry hole on the property of attorney Eck Brock. The ploy caused Standard Oil, according to Galbreath, to pay Brock way too much to lease the adjoining land.

And there was the time that he successfully challenged a judge who auctioned the allotments of Creek Indian children too cheaply due to inadequate advertising of the sale. The angered judge told Galbreath he would have to put up $30,000 in earnest money before he could bid at the new auction. A few hours later, Galbreath heaved gunny sacks full of money on the judge's bench.

Oh, there were lots of memories – the train ride with Governor Charles Haskell the night the Great Seal of Oklahoma was stolen, then moved by Model T from Guthrie to Oklahoma City (It was rumored that Charlie Colcord had a hand in that.); a chartered train Galbreath paid for so he and friends could attend the first inauguration of President Woodrow Wilson; the Tulsa parades, where he would load the family in their fancy automobile festooned with flowers and ribbons; the wonderful times at the family's summer retreat on an Iowa lake.

Shortly after 1912, with the discovery of the tremendous Cushing Field, Galbreath would seldom again be hailed as the *King of the Wildcatters*. That title would be handed to, and kept by, another gambler – Tom Slick.

But what happened to the Galbreath money? It is not entirely clear. Frank Galbreath, the Galbreaths' third child, provides a clue in his book, *Glenn Pool ...and a little oil town of yesteryear.*

The book was published in 1978, three years before Frank Galbreath died. It has been used for details and sequencing of events in this story.

Frank wrote that his father's friend Chesley became involved in a fire insurance company, which was deluged with claims. He said his father loaned Chesley $250,000, "on the cuff," to keep the insurance company afloat. That didn't do the trick, so Galbreath handed Chesley another $250,000. Finally, Galbreath took over the company and lost yet another quarter-million dollars.

Frank also wrote that the father-son conversation regarding these events occurred about 15 years later, "when, with a tank

Mary Ellen and Bob Galbreath with son Frank at Bromide, a health spa in southeastern Oklahoma. The spa, along with the Galbreath Hotel there, eventually failed.

full of gas in the old Model T and about fifty dollars of our own in our collective pockets, we were out getting a bloc of acreage together down in Coal County (southeastern Oklahoma)."

The son then asked his father why he loaned all that money to Chesley.

"Son, when we were drilling Glenn Number One, and supplies were short, Frank (Chesley) would walk all the way into Tulsa for groceries, load them on his shoulders, and walk all the way back again. He was a good ol' boy," Galbreath replied.

According to an article tucked inside a thick scrapbook in Kiefer City Hall, Chesley wandered here and there, wound up working as a janitor in Okmulgee, and died in 1924.

Frank Galbreath asked his father how much money he had on tap in the best of his years in the Glenn Pool.

"Son, I figure when I was going real good, I could have laid my hands on four or five or six million dollars," Galbreath replied.

The wildcatter's son said he never asked the question again, "Because a man with that much money, who allowed himself an explanatory spread of a couple million dollars, probably didn't know how much money he *did* have."

Like the great oil field itself, Galbreath would fade but not disappear. Down in southeastern Oklahoma near the border of Johnston and Coal counties, when Galbreath still had the funds, he built what he hoped would become a national health spa, based on the town of Bromide's natural springs bubbling with sulfur and bromide. He also established a rock quarry there, complete with a limestone crusher. The Galbreath Hotel emerged. Excursion trains arrived. Will Rogers even showed up, providing cracker-barrel philosophy and a few rope tricks for the guests.

But something strange happened. Common folks were buying automobiles – cheap automobiles. Henry Ford's Tin Lizzie, the Model T, allowed them to go wherever their balloon tires could take them. Business dropped off at Bromide. Then the Great Depression came, and the bottom fell out.

Always interested in politics, Galbreath ran for mayor of Tulsa in 1932, telling voters he had drilled a total of 132 wells in his lifetime, with but one duster. He ran on a campaign platform centered on his belief that Oklahoma Natural Gas was charging Tulsans too much. The election loss must have been both ironic and bitterly disappointing. In 1906 – the same year Oklahoma Natural Gas drew its first mighty breath by piping gas from the Glenn Pool toward Oklahoma City – Galbreath had obtained a potentially lucrative franchise to provide gas to Tulsa homes and businesses for 25 years. An ordinance, signed by Mayor John Mitchell, gave the wildcatter permission to use "all of the streets, alleys, public grounds and highways within the present and future city limits" to set up the new business.

Author Bob Gregory wrote in 1980 that *politics, shady dealings and dirty pool conspired against him.* The franchise, according to Gregory, soon slipped from Galbreath's grasp into the hands of none other than Glenn Braden, one of the founders of Oklahoma Natural Gas and the fellow who had earlier bought out Galbreath's gas interests in the Red Fork Field.

Galbreath liked no other man in Tulsa history less than Braden. They almost had a shotgun duel, at Galbreath's instigation, and he later much regretted that they hadn't, Gregory wrote.

The onetime *King of the Wildcatters* was a delegate to a couple of Democratic National Conventions, and unsuccessfully ran for Congress in 1944. He was 80 years old. His wife, Mary Ellen, that pretty little Irish girl who made the Land Run of '89, died the next year at age 72. She spent her last few months in a sanatorium near Tulsa. Their son Frank said her illness was brought on "partly by overwork in raising an active and turbulent family ..."

At the couple's fiftieth wedding anniversary, a few years earlier, her words to a *Tulsa Tribune* reporter reflected that her strong and upbeat personality had remained intact.

"We've learned that even if you do stumble now and then that you can always pick yourself up," Mary Ellen told the reporter. "And after you do that a few times, even the worst fall doesn't seem like much."

Almost as an afterthought at the end of the article, the reporter noted that Galbreath was *interested in mining properties in the southern part of the state.* Those few words essentially captured his life – always looking for the next big thing.

Galbreath spent his final years gardening – he is pictured doing so in a white shirt and a dark tie – and writing letters, to oilman and Senator Robert S. Kerr; to the Democrats' favorite son, Adlai Stevenson; to newspaper editors; to friends. He still had some fire in the belly and wasn't yet through with his war against Standard Oil and their ilk, referring to them as "second-handers." And he kept coming up with ideas for new ventures – a giant, underground bomb shelter being one, to protect West Tulsa refinery workers from the Cold War's potential Armageddon.

Recognized as Tulsa's *Grand Old Pioneer,* he withdrew from the International Petroleum Exposition's contest for the same title in 1953 due to failing health, mentioning that it was time for someone else to receive the honor. He died that December – 10 days short of his ninetieth birthday and his lucky number, twenty-two. A *Tulsa World* headline read:

Services Set Wednesday for Tulsa's 'King of the Wildcatters'

Galbreath would have liked that.

The year after his death, the Galbreaths' South Boulder mansion, used in its last years as a funeral home, was hauled away to make way for Warren Petroleum, which later would be sold to Gulf Oil. Bob and Mary Ellen had sold the home in 1919, moving to more modest surroundings.

And what of Bob and Ida Glenn? He bought a shiny new Model T in 1910, becoming one of 15 million to make just such a purchase during the car's long production run. When the discovery well had gurgled to life on their property five years earlier, there were only 75,000 automobiles in the entire country. Theirs came with a chauffeur to teach Bob Glenn how to drive the thing, with its three pedals and a hand-brake lever on the floor, and its throttle and spark advance on the column. Bravely setting out on his own with Ida and family aboard, he promptly ran into a telephone pole. The family walked the dusty half-mile back to their farm house in silence.

The Glenn family moved to Florida around 1915, then to Oregon, and finally down to Cayucos, California, where Ida died at age 83, Bob at 96. In the descriptive word of a niece, they had lived "sumptuously." The Glenn kids didn't do badly, either. Elena Glenn Page, a baby when the Ida Glenn well arrived, received a $43,000 bonus for the lease on her allotment – one of the highest amounts paid to a minor child.

Frank Galbreath, left, with officials at the 1972 unveiling of the Glenn Pool historical marker at the town of Glenpool.

With a Cast of Thousands

Boom-Time Dramas

On a polar-cold day on a hardscrabble farm in Ohio, Charlie Shobe was about to make a decision that would shape the rest of his life. So, too, were thousands of others – northeast to Pennsylvania and New York, south to deep Texas, and west as far as California.

Being attracted to a place they had only heard or read about but had never seen, they came in droves: speculators and field men; rig builders, drillers, roughnecks, roustabouts and shooters; teamsters, blacksmiths and machinists; tankies, welders and pipeliners; merchants of every stripe and supply-house sales-men; cooks and waitresses; gamblers and prostitutes; and, later, teachers and preachers.

Thousands had preceded and thousands more would follow Charlie Shobe's arrival at the Glenn Pool. Indian Territory and, soon, all of Oklahoma would never be quite the same after an oil field – on a scale never here before witnessed – quivered, shook, and boomed.

A relative few would become fabulously rich; more would go broke. Some would violently lose their lives. Most, like Charlie Shobe, came to make a better life for themselves and their families. Quietly and persistently, they would succeed.

"I was 31 years old, with a wife and four kids, and not getting anywhere – fast – back in Spencerville, Ohio," Shobe recalled. "It was the dead of winter when I got to talking to my friend and neighbor, Bob Gaberdiel.

"It was 26 degrees below zero, and there was fourteen inches of solid ice on the ground, with fresh snow falling fast. Our livestock already was thin and rough-coated. Our pocketbooks, like the livestock, were getting thinner by the day. We both knew we were in real trouble if spring was late in coming. It was 1907, and we were sure worried."

Charlie had heard about the Glenn Pool during the summer of 1906 while working for a fellow who had seen the field. The employer told him that a man could make as much as $150 a month there, and offered to write a letter of introduction to Franchot Oil. Now, in the dead of winter, Charlie turned to Gaberdiel with an idea.

"I've been thinking of going out there and working until May, anyway. As you know, we'll be froze up here that long. How about going with me, and we'll batch? We could live a lot cheaper that way. This feller says that board and room are sky high, a dollar a day."

"Well," said Gaberdiel, "I never thought of it, but I've been noticing in the papers about the big boom down there. The papers say they are going to make Indian Territory into a state – Oklahoma!"

"We thought it over and decided to go," Shobe said. "But at the house later, we were a pretty sober bunch of young folks as we talked over the arrangements that would have to be made. Bob's younger brother was to stay with his wife and take care of the livestock for both families. We agreed to pay him fifty cents a day."

Two days later, they boarded a train for Tulsa.

"Wagons, buggies, saddle ponies were tied up everywhere (in Tulsa), especially in front of the little brick bank. That bank was bulging with oil money. All over the whole country, from Tulsa toward the Glenn Pool, wagons loaded with oil-field supplies were moving or were stuck fast in the mud or deep sands of the Arkansas River bottoms," Shobe said.

The two farmers made their way to Kiefer, the hub of the activity.

"No one could tell you what Kiefer was like," Shobe said. "It seemed that confusion was everywhere. The khaki-clad, high-booted men who directed things seemed to know where they were going. The great masses of heavy wagons, pulled by teams of ten to twenty mules or horses, were going, or trying to go, in every direction. Utter confusion! Steam boilers, rig timbers, pipe, wooden tanks – all sorts of oil-field stuff were lining the muddy streets.

"Old Bob and I were sure out of our element, for we had never been anything but farmers. Now, suddenly, here we were smack-dab in the middle of the roughest and toughest oil town in the country. We felt like a couple of hillbillies in Times Square. The people, masses of them, surged back and forth, back and forth, on the dirt sidewalks and board porches fronting little stores, which had been thrown up to cater to the needs of thousands of people who had come here. One little store, and a post office tucked away in one corner of it, had been swallowed up in the maze of shacks nailed together in a matter of hours, almost. No one greeted us. No one even noticed us."

Shobe and Gaberdiel were awestruck. They stood motionless, trying to take it all in. After a time, their stomachs rumbled, reminding that they hadn't eaten all day. They found a restaurant and joined the "wall-standers" waiting for a sandwich and a cup of coffee. The winter light was fading when they realized they needed a place to sleep. A boarding house owner informed them, "Our

Oil field workers ate when and where they could – on the ground, at the back of buckboards, and under a circus tent. Farmers' wives often provided home-cooked meals for 25 cents apiece to the Glenn Pool oil hands.

rooms are taken by the week, and even if a fellow leaves, he has a dozen buddies waiting to take his place."

In darkness, they wandered from place to place. By sheer luck, they stumbled into the canvas-tent sleeping quarters of Franchot Oil. The rows of cots were full, but the oil-field workers placed one-by-twelve boards on the tent's dirt floor and offered the strangers a couple of blankets. Charlie and Bob slept soundly.

"Five o'clock came before I got straightened out," said Shobe, who met the boss at breakfast. Immediately, he and Gaberdiel had jobs. Shobe, with no training, became a pumper right there and then, tending to "thirty wells pouring a great, steady stream of oil into the big, old wooden tanks."

Everything went fine on his first day, until he was sent back across a frozen gully to gauge the tanks that night.

This peaceful scene of Kiefer is deceptive; it always was deadly dangerous and normally elbow-to-elbow busy during the oil boom.

"I broke through. I was plumb up to my knees in icy, muddy, oily slush. I scrambled wildly to gain my balance, and then, arms flailing, I went down. Mud, ice and slush went into my mouth, nose and ears. My hair and jacket and boots were full of the slimy stuff. I struggled up and, after using a few choice words not meant for ladies' ears, I went back to camp.

"I slept soundly, thinking the boss would never know I had not made my rounds. But he knew all right! The whole camp knew!"

The tanks had overflowed during the night, sending thousands of barrels of crude to the frozen ground.

"It's hard to believe," Shobe would recall decades after the incident, "but I just never realized the tanks would fill and run over."

Franchot Oil, like dozens of other companies furiously working the field, needed every man it could find. The lease boss figured Shobe to be someone who had made a mistake, nothing more and nothing less. He was given a second chance, but warned that he would be sent packing if one more tank overflowed.

Shobe and Gaberdiel both wanted out of Kiefer. With their first pay, they ordered a tent from a Montgomery Ward catalogue and waited for its arrival amidst the tons of goods and equipment coming by rail every day from near and far.

"We picked it up a week later from Red Fork, borrowed a lease team (of horses), and set up the tent in a grove of trees (outside Kiefer)," he said.

Flour sacks filled with hay served as pillows; a straw tick filled with the same provided their new mattresses on rusty bed frames. A coal-oil lamp and granite pots and pans rounded out their new belongings. They felt like they had it made.

These were basically hardworking, honest men who epitomized the heartbeat of the field. Unlike many who were on their own and away from their

Former Ohio farmers Bob Gaberdiel and Charlie Shobe (seated from left) thought they had it made after their Montgomery Ward tent arrived, allowing them to move from wild-and-wooly Kiefer to the countryside.

families, they avoided the rotgut whisky, the gambling, the carousing, and the fighting, all of which became legendary around the field in general, at Kiefer in particular.

"When we first hit Kiefer," Shobe recalled, "there seemed to be not so much meanness as came later. Then, killings, muggings, holdups and robberies got to be expected almost every night for two or three years. It wasn't safe to be in a dark place anywhere or at any time on Kiefer's main street."

As darkness descended, proper, fearful women stayed inside tents or tiny, wooden homes – called shotguns, because a blast could go straight through the place when the front and back doors were opened. Many of the tents were transformed to shotgun houses over a period of time, with a wooden floor being added first, then wooden sides, and finally a permanent roof. Children played within the oil-camp confines of what their parents deemed safe. Lawmen, with no credentials except for a readiness to use fists and revolvers, were viewed suspiciously and given a broad path.

On numerous occasions, men walking home from a night on the town were, at best, relieved of their money and sent on their way. At worst, they were beaten or killed. The robberies, beatings and killings frequently occurred on a wooden-plank bridge spanning a slough, but weren't limited to it. The casual attitude that prevailed toward such violence is made apparent by the experience of a young boy who would spend his life in the oil fields.

Cliff Mefford awoke one morning, stepped outside, and saw a body lying in the narrow pathway between two houses. Speechless, he pointed to the body as the town marshal approached.

"I know, sonny. He's been lying there all night. I've just been too busy to get around to him," the marshal said.

Eventually, three deputies were sent from Tulsa to bring the Kiefer situation under control.

"One of them was a pretty fair hand at gambling, I reckon, for he sure made a killing at the gambling joint one dark night," Shobe said. "Then, with only a pale moon for light, he started across the old plank walk, knowing the other two marshals were hidden at each end."

The deputy saw a masked robber approach him from the far end of the makeshift bridge. Another masked man closed in from behind. Just as the deputy was ordered to surrender the winnings, his fellow lawmen rushed to make the arrests.

Shobe said removal of the masks revealed that the robbers were Kiefer's top lawman and his sidekick, who were tied to an oak tree before being hauled off to the tiny jail in Red Fork.

Kiefer's legendary rough-and-tumble past is painted most graphically by an anonymous driller, interviewed by Ned DeWitt

Wooden derricks and steel storage tanks spread through the Glenn Pool as quickly as money, manpower and material allowed.

and recorded in *Voices from the Oil Fields,* edited by Paul Lambert and Kenny Franks.

"There were fights and killings every day. You got used to seeing them," said the driller, who related the fate of a friend who was innocently watching a fight on the notorious bridge.

"A Dutch boy with us got so excited he got right on the edge of the bank and was cheering them on, when one bird climbed out and took a whack at Dutchie with a board he'd yanked off the bridge, and knocked him in the creek. We waded in after him, after knocking this guy and a couple more out of the way, and picked up Dutch and took him back to his room and then sent for a doc. Dutch had a fractured skull. He died before they got him back home in Wisconsin."

Much of the Kiefer violence brewed in the Mad House saloon, according to the driller, where payoffs to law officers were part of everyday business.

"The little creek that ran through the town was chock-full of stiffs, and every time the oil was skimmed off the top so you could see the water, there'd be a body float up to the top. Some of the first steel tanks I ever saw were there, big fifty-five-thousand-barrel steel ones like we've got today, and they had gates on the ladders leading up to the top so nobody could get up there at night and stick a hose in and steal the oil.

"Several times, they noticed that the lock had been busted off the gate, and there was blood on the ladder of the big tank right back of the Mad House. They didn't think much about it, till one day the company decided there was so much sludge in the bottom of the tank they'd have to clean it out. They drained all the oil off and found seven skeletons down in the mess on the bottom," the driller said.

The parents of one of the victims identified their son by his dental work. To their shock and horror, they realized that someone had attempted to pry out their boy's gold fillings.

For all the tales of violence – there are dozens – good men and good families lived in and around the Glenn Pool. They avoided the dangers, gloried in the adventure. There was an element of enticing romance, which is reflected by Charlie Shobe's prose-like, nighttime view:

"Gas flares, burning in the air, made weird, flickering lights over the rolling hills and valleys. The old, wooden rigs and their derricks looked like the fabled Dragon's Teeth in the story of *Jason and the Golden Fleece*."

Shobe's wife, Lillie Belle, and their four children joined him in the summer of 1907, moving into a new shotgun house

Charlie had built. Shobe would pump the same lease for 30 years – never once letting another tank overflow.

Harry Shobe, a Sapulpa glass plant worker, says his grand-father wound up buying the 80 acres he pumped.

"He farmed and pumped oil," Harry says. "He owned the first ice plant in Kiefer, and he owned a service station or two. He was a good and honest man – no nonsense. He wasn't afraid to do anything."

A couple of other farmer-rancher types, Robert McFarlin and James Chapman, also would return to their roots, but their spreads would be measured in tens of thousands of acres. (See *Characters and Kind Hearts.*)

Charlie Shobe died on April 1, 1964. He was 89, the same age as Bob Galbreath, the wildcatter who discovered the field. Shobe told his story to his daughter, Effah Ward, and to Olivia Myers. Charlie's story is recorded in a two-set volume of Creek County family recollections published by the Sapulpa Historical Society.

BEFORE THE BEGINNING

The Glenn Pool didn't originate in a total vacuum. Before the oil was discovered, the field was surrounded by towns striving for growth during a time when success amounted to having water – hopefully somewhat drinkable water – and being in the path of at least one railroad, shipping out cattle and bringing in goods, equipment and newcomers.

There was a growing awareness of oil in Indian Territory, which encompassed the eastern half of Oklahoma. From 1891 to

1905 in Indian and Oklahoma territories, no fewer than 19 discoveries had occurred in unproven fields. All but four of these were within 70 miles of the future greatest oil field in America.

Each discovery was like a stone plunked into a pond, the ripples of awareness extending outward, leading to more wildcat attempts. The Glenn Pool would be the first boulder, sending out tidal waves.

Towns such as Kiefer and Glenpool rose up directly and entirely from the massive demands of the oil field. A few others did, too, but they would vanish in the hard times by or before the Great Depression a quarter-century distant from the discovery. By default of proximity, Kiefer would be the epicenter.

To the south was Mounds, to the west, Sapulpa. Jenks, Red Fork and Tulsa were to the north. None was ready, could possibly have been prepared, for the great boom.

Mounds kept settling down in the wrong place – not once, not twice, but three times. The town originally was built between a pair of soft-edged upheavals known as Twin Mounds in anticipation of the Texas-bound Battle Axe Railroad. Townspeople waited and waited, but the railroad was never built. To their consternation, they learned that the railroad's president had been sent to prison for using government money to build the rail beds.

Their spirits lifted, however, as the Frisco extended its lines from Sapulpa into Texas in 1899. Soon, they moved the entire town over to that railroad line. Mike Glenn, brother of Bob Glenn, had barely finished unloading the wooden buildings and homes when it became clear that the town was a smidgen too close to Drake Switch, according to Frisco regulations. It would build no depot at Mounds.

Drake Switch was nothing more than a flag station, where passenger trains whizzed by nonstop unless telegraphed to pick up riders; and freight trains stopped only if a white flag was waving. Railroad men occasionally bedded down in a boxcar there on the little siding.

Undeterred, Mounds called on Mike's strong back, his rugged team of horses, and his sturdy wagon to move the town again, farther down the rails. That accomplished, all of Mounds let out a collective sigh of relief, nested in, and prospered on the rolling prairie.

Years later, as the Glenn Pool drilling fanned out from the discovery well, folks realized they had moved away from the oil. Drake Switch was renamed Kiefer.

"If Mounds hadn't moved, Glenpool and Kiefer wouldn't have existed," says Michelle Thomas, president of the Mounds Historical Society.

Yet another twist of fate also became evident as the oil field developed. In the town's ongoing efforts to settle in the "right" place, its original 80 acres had been swapped for the like-size federal allotment of Creek Indian Maxwell Corbett. Royalties received for production on his new land made him wealthy.

As for "Mike-the-mover," he took such a liking to Mounds that he spent the rest of his life right there.

"After hoisting the buildings around so much, I got sort of attached to the place," he said.

At pre-boom Jenks, boosters set up a risky steamboat ride down the Arkansas River. The arriving excursionists were offered town lots – land formerly owned by three ex-slave freedmen – for 25 bucks. Each buyer got a "free" share in an oil venture, which came up drier than the Arkansas River that summer afternoon in 1905. Would-be lot buyers made the trip back to Tulsa on the Midland Valley Railway.

Sapulpa had grown steadily since greeting its first train in 1886. It had a two-story brick courthouse, a high school, hotels, banks, a variety of stores, library and a literary club – all the trappings of a good town. Named for Creek Indian Chief James Sapulpa, hailed as its first permanent set-

A low flying bird's-eye view of Sapulpa, circa 1902.

tler, it engaged Tulsa in a years-long rivalry, which intensified after the Glenn Pool strike.

Several more-distant towns — Muskogee, Okmulgee, Claremore and Vinita — were bigger and far better than Tulsa. But Tulsa paid no mind to such annoying facts. A public-relations marvel, it bragged on everything and admitted nothing.

Tulsans turned on its head the time-honored concept that improvements bring growth. It explained why an opera house – something to brag about – was built, its builder enticed with a $6,000 bonus, before the first muddy street was paved or a decent water system was planned. (The city didn't have a really good water supply of its own until 1924, when the ingenious Spavinaw Lake system was implemented through construction of a dam, a series of pipelines some 60 miles long, and a water-treatment plant.

President Calvin Coolidge threw the switch that started the water flowing.)

Tulsa leaders were brash and overly confident, with a peculiar, self-deprecating sense of humor. When its people grew tired of smelling or sliding into a ditch filled with raw sewage from the Robinson Hotel, they organized a protest. The hotel responded by dumping the stuff directly into the Arkansas River and staging a "sewer banquet" for the miffed protesters.

Buoyed by the effects of their $50,000 river crossing – immodestly but accurately dubbed the "bridge that saved Tulsa" – they set out to lure settlers by methods undreamed of by towns grounded in reality and practicality. Such common sense was foreign to the eager-beaver boosters known as the Commercial Club, forerunner to the Chamber of Commerce.

A *Joplin Globe* reporter wrote such a glowing article that it pleased even the good ol' boys of the club. He was impressed by the number of railroads serving Tulsa, noting that town boosters had given them a total of $37,000 in "bonuses" – described as bribes by Sapulpans and other critics.

The 1904 toll "bridge that saved Tulsa."

The bridge's only competition: ferries.

Tulsa's railroad courtships were remarkable. From 1901, when the Red Fork Field was discovered, to pre-Glenn Pool 1905, the Commercial Club persuaded and influenced the Katy, the Midland Valley and the Santa Fe to build their lines of commerce through the town.

For example, when the boosters learned that a proposed Santa Fe line from Bartlesville to Muskogee would bypass them, they mapped out plans for their own railroad line. Amazed and threatened, Santa Fe capitulated, constructing the line through pipsqueak Tulsa.

Similarly, the Midland Valley planned to erect a terminal in Red Fork but was "induced" to build it in Tulsa. And when officials of the Frisco, which first chugged into Tulsa in 1882, said they were about to build a branch from Sapulpa to Enid, Tulsa boosters again prevailed, persuading them, instead, to originate it from their town.

The Commercial Club guys had no idea yet, but the railroads, particularly the Frisco and Midland Valley, would be vital, life-giving arteries in the coming oil boom.

Only months before the Ida Glenn well gurgled, spit and shot to life 14 miles south of Tulsa, 100 members of the Commercial Club pitched in $100 apiece to charter a train to carry them and their southern-preacher-like zeal to dozens of Midwest towns and cities. When the train headed out of town, it carried 80 businessmen, a band, a trick-roper named Bill Rogers, and a printing press borrowed from the *Tulsa Democrat*.

The boosters telegraphed newspapers and Commercial Clubs along the route. The missives made it clear that they were coming to "induce a few hundred men of money to locate in the greatest city in the world."

Tulsa's legitimate population, perhaps 5,000, and its attributes grew at every stop, where fresh "news" rolled off the little printing press.

By chowder, ain't you never heard of Tulsa? Sorry for your ignorance. Why Tulsa's got seven churches and no saloons. A man can clear up to six-hundred dollars a year there, easy. Got a natural gas belt that's as big an' active as our hot-air department.

Tulsa in 1893, long before the chest-thumping began.

All hell broke loose in Chicago, to the great delight of the boosters. When they refused Pullman's pleas to remove their billowing, car-side banners, Chicago's finest responded, trailed by newspaper reporters. When they arrived, band members were playing a ragged medley of tunes atop the Pullman car.

At the Chicago Mercantile Exchange, the band marched onto the floor, where Rogers lassoed a herd of traders. "It was one of the first cases of me and my little rope making a public appearance," he said after becoming better known as Will Rogers, Oklahoma's cowboy philosopher, humorist and syndicated columnist.

The trip exceeded the boosters' wildest dreams. Through personal contact, newspaper articles and word-of-mouth, people from Vancouver to New York came to Tulsa just to see for themselves what kind of place could breed such enthusiasm.

Tulsa's effervescent, anything's-possible, sky's-the-limit attitude was perfect for the coming oil boom.

No Instant 'Ka-boom'

In the mind's eye, the words *oil boom* convey immediacy; a sea of derricks; commotion and confusion; trains bringing passengers and oil-field material to the depots; freight-bearing wagons strung out for miles; enormous growth and change. Certainly, this accurately describes Charlie Shobe's Glenn Pool, but activity during the field's first months was far from boom pace. Only a few wells were drilled, and the first oil didn't make its way out of the field until mid-spring of 1906.

According to the *Tulsa World,* established two months before the Glenn Pool discovery, J. C. Eldred and M. H. Mosier were drilling west of the Glenn farm when the original Ida Glenn well came in. Their well flowed 75 barrels a day, but there was no immediate roar of publicity or rush to develop the field in the wake of two modestly successful wells.

In mid-February, nearly three months after the Glenn Pool discovery, Standard Oil completed a pipeline from Red Fork to the field. The pipe's diameter, about the size of a car's tailpipe, indicated that Standard Oil's commitment was limited, but the elephant had its nose under the tent.

At this same time, the *Mounds Enterprise* reported that the Frisco had delivered equipment and tools for six derricks. A smattering of oilmen began arriving to determine for themselves whether this was a flash in the pan or the beginning of a bona fide oil field. They had no idea that it would, for a time, overpower all the storage tanks, rail-loading facilities and pipelines built to accommodate it.

In March, Bob Galbreath made another strike 300 feet from his discovery well, whose oil still hadn't made it out of the field. Ida Glenn No. 2 flowed mightily at first, then settled in at 800 barrels a day, more than nine times the discovery well's production. (All wells on the farm were named Ida Glenn, with numbers signifying the order of their arrival. This practice occurred on all the leases.)

The busy little *Mounds Enterprise* reported that another well, on a nearby farm, came in about this time. It supposedly was the first well "shot" with nitroglycerin, an extremely volatile explosive that creates channels in the sandstone formation, allowing the oil to flow more copiously.

The arrival of the shooter in late March signaled the entry of a breed of men looked upon by oil-field regulars with awe and wonderment – awe regarding the power packed by the quart cans of nitroglycerin "soup" lowered into the wells and detonated; wonderment at how anyone could be crazy enough to take on such a job.

There were only two types of shooters: the ones who had made a mistake and the ones who hadn't – yet. Every time a horse-drawn soup wagon hit a rut, took a big bounce, a real chance surfaced for the whole batch to explode. Signs that a wagon hadn't made it to a designated well amounted to a crater in the earth and bits of horseflesh. That being the case, another soup wagon and another shooter were irreverently sent to the job site.

Although many were true, shooter stories emerging from the Glenn Pool and successive Oklahoma fields became folklore.

Folks gave the well-paid shooters a wide berth – and with good reason.

A roughneck lost his head when parts from the derrick sliced through the tree he was hiding behind. A baby, eating Post Toasties in her highchair, was spared, not a hair on her head injured, when an entire magazine exploded, sending a steel door ripping through the length of the house, knocking away the cereal bowl.

After automobiles became commonplace, one shooter put a siren and air horn on his converted, literally "souped-up" Cadillac.

"When I wanted the way cleared, I'd open up on the siren and give them the horn to boot. (When) I got close to a town, I'd always let them beller, and people would stop and stare at me till I was up close enough they could read the big, red danger signs on the sides; then they'd run like chickens." *(Voices from the Oil Fields.)*

Nearly all of the oil-field jobs were dangerous. When a man was injured, he was patched up and, if humanly possible, returned to work. There were no unemployment, workers compensation or welfare checks waiting in the mail. Rig-builder Charlie Storms watched as a doctor dipped common pliers into alcohol and pulled down the severed tendons from his leg, which had been severely injured in a saw-blade mishap. The tendons were joined and knotted together.

"That old fool tied those leaders in square knots so they couldn't slip or break, and they pulled my heel clean back against my ankle. I couldn't walk a step," Storms said. "He told me to get a wood block to use for a high heel for that foot, and every little while to shave off a piece. I did, but it was over a year before I could walk again." *(Voices from the Oil Fields)*

In April, a well on Eck Brock's allotment sent gas rocketing past the "black dogs," coal-oil lamps dangling from iron rods on the derrick. The fumes ignited, destroying the rig and seriously burning driller Frank McGuinn. The accident was remarkable only in that he survived and that it was the first fire in the Glenn Pool. Dozens more would follow.

In May, almost six months after the field's discovery, five wells were now producing on the Glenn farm alone. Combined with rapidly appearing other wells, the field reportedly was producing much of all the oil produced in Indian Territory, according to the *Mounds Enterprise,* which guesstimated the field's production at 30,000 barrels a day – probably way high. However, wells producing 1,000 barrels per day were becoming the rule.

Much greater "naturals" – wells unaided by nitroglycerin blasts – would be reported later in the year, including several in the

4,000-barrel range. The first of those was on the Nevada Berryhill lease, which unleashed fortunes. A few wells came in as high as 5,000 barrels, but didn't maintain that level.

In mid June, a 20-million-cubic-foot gasser blew in on the west side of the Glenn farm. Reported as the strongest flow of gas in the entire Mid-Continent Region, it provided cheap fuel for nearly all the rigs, which had relied on coal and wood to fuel their boilers.

By late summer, the Glenn Pool was growing quickly. Twenty-three wells, two of them gassers, were producing. Every day saw at least one new well completed, sometimes two or three. The field was about two miles long and a mile wide, or approximately 1,280 acres. Several dozen cable-tool rigs were pounding their bits into the Bartlesville sand and the hydrocarbon treasure held tightly for eons.

WHOSE FIELD IS IT, ANYWAY?

Although the field's importance and potential were becoming more evident, its name was up for grabs. Tulsa and Sapulpa each desperately wanted its name attached, and Mounds wanted both to butt out. At stake were bragging rights and hoped-for fame and fortune.

The *Sapulpa Light* accused Tulsans of "claiming everything within 50 miles" and continually "bubbling off," claiming that newcomers were getting tired of their hot air.

Such criticism served only to invigorate the *Tulsa Democrat*, which claimed that its city would become "quite an oil center." The newspaper took note of Tulsa's four railroads, its hotels and other accommodations, adding that the "Oil Well Supply Company and the National Supply Company are planning to make Tulsa a base."

That was actually news, a serious blow to Sapulpa, which later would attract its own oil-supply house, Pennsylvania-bred Bovaird, for a $7,000 bonus. The *Tulsa Democrat* rubbed salt in the wound by under-reporting Sapulpa's population and claiming that it was "only a Frisco division point" – a one-trick pony – where "the oil atmosphere does not settle about the town gracefully." (Sapulpa was justifiably proud of its Frisco division headquarters, and Tulsa knew it. The railroad payroll there grew to be a million dollars. In 1927, the division would move to Tulsa; Sapulpa treated the event as nothing less than grand theft.)

The *Mounds Enterprise* urged Tulsa and Sapulpa to "quit arguing about our oil field."

To his everlasting credit, wildcatter Galbreath insisted that the field be named in honor of Bob and Ida Glenn, whom he considered friends. Their name gradually settled in on the field. On July 3, 1906, when the *Oil Investors' Journal* down in Beaumont, Texas, finally took notice of the field, it was called the Glenn Wells.

RICH KIDS AND $100 DOLLS

Lease agents, commonly referred to as landmen, scoured the countryside in all directions from the Glenn farm that first summer. Available land was becoming scarce, and lease prices were rising exponentially. Land had been leased for as little as a buck-fifty-five an acre in the early going, before the clamor commenced. The price of a lease was directly linked to how close the land was to a successful well, how many barrels that well was producing, and how much cash the oil operators had to spare.

One lease agent claimed that $2.5 million had been offered for a parcel and was turned down cold. That sounds incredible until you consider that several of the top leases would gross $1 million or more in oil revenues in their first full year of production.

The lease agents ranged from honest businessmen looking out for the interests of their bosses to outright crooks. The Interior Department provided some protection for the Creek Indians involved, with all leases requiring its approval, and all payments being routed through its Muskogee office and then on to the allottees. Local judges presided over lease activities involving Creek Indian children, a number of whom became rich overnight from bonuses paid separately from the production royalty payments mandated by the Interior Department's Office of Indian Affairs.

The Interior Department provided no such protection to freedmen, who also were allotted land. As a result, they were more vulnerable to unscrupulous deal-makers.

The hatched up scheme of a Muskogee lawyer and a Mounds farmer gained them title to a 120-acre tract of land in the Glenn Pool for $800. The lawyer was representing a freedman in jail, and the Mounds farmer happened to know about some unclaimed land in the Glenn Pool. They put up $400 apiece, freed the freedman, and instructed him how to file for the 160-acre tract. They "let" him keep 40 acres. It isn't known how much money his new "friends" made.

Another freedman, Zeke Moore, found himself in the hoosegow on charges of horse theft. After he was released, he could buy all the horses he wanted – $400,000 in royalty checks had accumulated for him at the Interior Department's Muskogee office.

The oil-rich or land-poor fate of the Creek Indians and the freedmen entirely hinged on where their allotments were. Royalties were still being paid out on some of the original leases in 2005.

In June of 1906, bonuses totaling more than $70,000 were paid to no fewer than 21 Creek Indian boys and girls. Lena Posey received $475, her brother, Boyse, $400, his being the lowest amount. Elena Glenn, from the discovery-well farm, at first received $16,000. A Sapulpa judge deemed that figure too small, on grounds that the Glenn farm already was home to several excellent producers. A new auction was held, rewarding the child with $43,000. Her income from royalties during the first full year of her lease exceeded that of her parents, Bob and Ida Glenn.

Other children receiving substantial bonuses that month included Edith Durant, $16,800 from one company and $2,000 from another; Joseph Berryhill, $12,600; Lona Love Perryman, $9,000; and Ralph Perryman, $4,625.

Six oil companies paid out June's $70,000-plus in bonuses; wildcatter Galbreath paid out $45,835 of the total.

In another auction, Earl Berryhill, barely 3 years old, drew $25,000. Five-year-old Robert Pittman Jr., who lived down the road from Elena Glenn, received a $49,000 bonus, the record amount.

Merchants began catering to the Creek Indians' deepening pockets. A Sapulpa storekeeper stocked a hundred-dollar porcelain doll imported from Germany. Each time one was pulled from the glass case for an Indian girl, another doll was ordered.

Tom Gilcrease was 15 when the Ida Glenn was discovered. Number 1505 on the Creek Indian rolls, he used a small portion of his $12,000 bonus to attend Bacone, an Indian-oriented college in Muskogee. The son of a Mounds cotton gin operator, he became wealthy from his quarter-section at the southern edge of the field.

Oilman and Mounds supporter W. H. Milliken drilled 40 wells there – one for every four acres – grossing $900,000 in one year and netting young Gilcrease $90,000. At 30 cents a barrel – reported as the average price for Glenn Pool crude from 1906 through 1910 – three million barrels were required to provide those figures.

Tom Gilcrease

(No oil was ever found on land owned by Gilcrease's kin-folks. Its absence testified as to just how tricky and unpredictable the Bartlesville sandstone formation could be. Oil found at one site was nowhere to be found only 300 feet away. Drilling occurred in all directions from the discovery well, but most of the few easterly attempts came up dry. It would be learned that the Bartlesville sand, sometimes referred to as the Glenn sand, essentially pinched out where U.S. Highway 75 now is. This formation, up to 240 feet thick, produced 90 percent or more of the field's entire oil production, usually at depths from 1,400 to 1,600 feet – but with many exceptions. Some oil also was found in the deeper

Wilcox sand, slightly beyond 2,000 feet.)

Gilcrease twice traveled to Europe, where he became interested in art. He wouldn't be inspired to gather the favored Old Masters, but would choose, instead, to collect American cowboy and Indian art, long before it was fashionable to do so.

He married and divorced twice, the second time around to 1927 Miss America Norma Smallwood of Tulsa. The oilman moved to San Antonio in 1949, displaying his growing collection on two floors of his office building. Feeling that it wasn't really appreciated there, he returned to Tulsa, placing the collection in buggy-carriage sheds and garage buildings.

For years, he was mired in legal entanglements with other oil companies involving his allotted land near Mounds. Deeply in debt, he pondered selling his collection, which now included thousands of paintings, drawings and prints, more than 50,000 artifacts, and a like number of books. By bond-issue vote, Tulsans bought it all for $2.25 million in 1954.

Gilcrease lived the last eight years of his life in a modest house at the museum overlooking the Osage Hills northwest of Tulsa. He continued collecting art and left it to the institution. Revenue from his oil properties, dedicated as a part of his original agreement with Tulsa, have exceeded the purchase price. The museum bearing his name houses the world's greatest Western art collection – one of many legacies traceable to the Glenn Pool.

Too Much, Too Soon

The producers faced a vexing problem, which worsened with every well completed: What were they going to do with all the oil?

The Glenn Pool's rapidly increasing volumes demanded adequate gathering systems, storage tanks, railroad loading facilities and, most importantly, pipelines to refineries. Making the problem more acute was this simple fact: The oil was in a pre-statehood, largely ungoverned and undeveloped territory with precious few resources to accommodate the field's gargantuan requirements.

Of course, the oil operators could have stopped drilling and waited for the infrastructure to catch up with production – and cows could have sprouted wings and flown to the moon.

A wise and wealthy operator would have built millions of barrels of storage, pumped them full, and waited patiently for crude-oil prices to rise – which they would, eventually. That's exactly what Harry Sinclair did, but very few had his brains and money. (See *Characters and Kind Hearts*.)

Companies with money built 55,000-barrel steel tanks; others made do with wooden tanks or simply flowed their crude into huge earthen pits.

Nearly all of the operators felt pressure to keep drilling as furiously as possible, which is exactly what they did. Some wells *were* stopped just short of the pay zone, some production actually *was* shut in, but these actions were few and far between.

Derricks in the Glenn Pool outstretched the eye's reach.

Producers needed to recoup their expenses, which were considerable, with each completed well costing $5,000 or more. Like cheerleaders from the sidelines, landowners were eager to start and keep receiving their royalty checks. Also, the Interior Department supposedly required drilling to commence within 90 days of each lease it approved.

For decades, oil exploration in this country was governed by a centuries-old English edict known as the "law of capture." If a bird from a neighboring estate happened to fly onto your land, go ahead and shoot – the bird is yours. Translated to the Glenn Pool, it meant that any oil that "happened" to flow underground from one lease to another was fair game. The nagging fear that one man's oil would be drained by another man's well served as a powerful impetus to keep the stuff flowing at all costs.

The science of petroleum geology – still in its infancy, its value questioned and sometimes ridiculed – wasn't used to develop this field. Instead, it was "close is best." An operator figured he was close enough to drill when he could smell oil from the competitor's well.

As a result of all these influences, wells were spaced far too tightly; from a distance they appeared to be almost on top of each other. So-called "line fights" were common, with competing operators squaring off against each other, building rigs at a frantic pace not more than 150 feet from the section-line roads.

Rig-builders were in extreme demand. They returned to their tents or wooden homes exhausted. There, a friend or a wife pulled deeply-implanted splinters from their hands. They never felt a thing – their hands were too calloused.

In innumerable cases, the Glenn Pool was a learn-as-you-go training school. Operators learned that a skilled carpenter doesn't equate to a good rig-builder. A carpenter's finished work might look good, but that didn't mean it was safe or that it would operate properly.

Two-by-twelve boards were tested by putting one end on the derrick floor, the other end on the shoulder of a man standing on the ground. Then, another man jumped on the board twice, once on each end. This way, good boards were separated from bad, which could mean the difference between life and death on a working rig with highly tensioned cable tools weighing thousands of pounds.

Just getting to the rigs often posed the biggest challenge of the day. Mounds, Sapulpa and Tulsa graded miles of roads, barely passable, to ensure that their links to the field were established and maintained. The roads – a kind term – were either choked with dust, mired in mud or iced over, depending on Ma Nature. There were no tow trucks or automobile clubs to call; axle-deep wagons were pulled to freedom by raw horsepower.

Demand for storage tanks grew with every well completion. Beginning in the summer of 1906, tankies would construct more than 14 million barrels of storage, with most of it up by late fall the

The oil-laden earthen pits appeared as dark lakes – deadly to waterfowl.

next year – an amazing accomplishment. By comparison, when Standard Oil had controlled most of the oil in Kansas at the turn of the century, its total storage capacity there was seven million barrels.

Tanks rose up around all sides of Jenks except along the Arkansas River to the east. Well-paid tankies and their families established homes there. Elsewhere, the wooden and steel vessels appeared on farms, giving coinage to the term *tank farms*.

The tankies were one of a kind, as tough as any man who ever put on a pair of work boots. As they rapidly aged, veins on their faces and limbs broke and their arms and legs bowed out from the stress of carrying heavy plates of steel. Intestinal ruptures were commonplace. The tops of their heads were ridged with burr-like, hair-erasing scars – battle wounds of the job.

Their work ethic and their willingness to mix it up were the stuff of legends. In the summer of 1907, when the mercury stayed above the century mark for two weeks straight in the middle of a drought, they worked until they passed out, falling face first. When they came to, they went back to work.

(In the Cushing Field following the Glenn Pool boom, tankies were kicked out of a little shack-town when they claimed that a gambling joint was crooked. They gathered up their fellow tank-builders the next day and literally tore the town to pieces, throwing the remains and "the punks" into the Canadian River.)

Companies with money and clout could obtain the labor and material required to build the steel tanks. Smaller operators either couldn't afford to build them or had trouble getting material. The operator on the Gilcrease lease ordered a pair of the largest tanks, graded areas for them, and waited in vain for the steel. Reluctantly, he diked the sites and began flowing his wells into them.

The largest of the earthen pits contained 200,000 barrels. These "lakes" proved deadly to waterfowl. It was rumored that ducks falling prey to the reservoirs, appearing from a distance as inviting ponds, wound up on the dinner plates of several restaurants. Cows, their mouths full of oil, drowned in oil-filled creeks stretching for miles.

Fires, a constant threat, increased in size as tanks and earthen dikes of oil were ignited by a variety of sources

Crowds invariably turned out to view the big fires, few of which were extinguished.

ranging from a welder's torch to electrical storms. Massive black clouds belched from burning tank fires, drawing spectators from miles around. On at least one lease, a Civil War cannon was kept handy so it could blow a hole through a blazing tank, allowing thousands of barrels of oil to escape before being consumed by the fire.

Polecat Creek, its water topped with oil, was afire day and night during the worst of these times. An estimated 5,000 barrels were lost – every day – to the combined effect of fires, evaporation, seepage, leaks and spills. Five-thousand barrels a day amounted to 1.8 million barrels a year. One of the largest operators claimed that he could have "saved" 40,000 barrels a day during peak production if adequate storage had been available.

The truth is, no one knows how much oil was lost during the field's early years.

On at least two occasions, severe windstorms toppled dozens of derricks. After the second round, steel derricks began appearing. The last wooden derrick, east of Kiefer, disappeared in the 1970s.

It was estimated that several billion cubic feet of natural gas had either been used as fuel for lighting and drilling or vented and flared by 1912. By then, small natural-gasoline plants, which stripped the liquids from the gas, were operating throughout the field. Franchot Oil, the company Charlie Shobe went to work for, built the first casing-head natural gas plant west of the Mississippi in 1909. Today, there is virtually no natural gas in the field. Water now does what natural gas used to do, forcing the oil to the surface. For every barrel of oil produced, 99 barrels of water come with it. The oil is separated from the water, which is re-injected into the field. The electric bill on 100 wells pumping out about 300 barrels a day is at least $60,000 a month.

The Silver Lining

Oilmen, by their very nature, are always looking for a silver lining but are not surprised when the entire sky crashes down on them. By the fall of 1906, Glenn Pool operators badly needed a remedy for their untenable storage and takeaway problems. Constantly, these men hoped for higher prices for their crude. They came to believe that their silver lining appeared in the immense, dark cloud hanging over Spindletop, the Texas oil field south of Beaumont. Spindletop became a monstrous field after it roared to life in 1901, but it had faltered, threatening the well-financed refineries built to accommodate its once seemingly endless supply of crude.

In its heyday, an acre of land at Big Hill had sold for as much as $900,000, the equivalent of $17 million in today's money, and Beaumont's population had swelled from 10,000 to 50,000. Those heady times were long gone in 1906. (The crest of the salt dome had produced some 60 million barrels. A rebirth of the field occurred on its flanks in 1917, producing a similar amount over a period of years.)

Referring to Big Hill's flush production from too many wells spaced too closely together, Patillo Higgins, a one-armed mechanic whose decade-long dream and persistence led to the Spindletop discovery, dryly observed: "They milked the cow too hard."

It would become an apt description of the Glenn Pool.

Gulf Refining and the Texas Company, renamed Texaco in '06 and given the famous star logo, began looking hundreds of miles north to the Glenn Pool as their salvation. This was particularly true of Gulf, which faced the real possibility of folding if it

Refineries built at Port Arthur, Texas, by Gulf Oil and the Texas Company were in response to the Spindletop discovery near Beaumont. As Spindletop's production sputtered and the Glenn Pool boomed, the two companies raced to complete pipelines linking the Oklahoma field to those distant refineries. Shown here is the Texas Company refinery in 1901, four years before the Glenn Pool rumbled to life.

didn't find new sources of crude for its Port Arthur refinery, built so large that it was capable of handling nearly all the oil Texas was producing at the time.

Although they didn't know – couldn't know – how much the Glenn Pool was capable of producing, they knew that its quality far surpassed that of Spindletop, or any other Texas oil field, for that matter. Some of Spindletop's asphalt-laden oil was of such poor quality it couldn't be refined. Glenn Pool oil was made up of smaller, lighter molecules, less asphalt, less sulfur – a refiner's dream. Kerosene, still the number-one revenue generator; gasoline; and a widening variety of products could be refined more quickly and more cheaply from the Glenn Pool crude. It was, in fact, as good as any oil west of the Appalachians.

(Such oil would become known worldwide as Oklahoma Light Sweet Crude, denoting that it is low in asphalt and sulfur content. Glenn Pool oil continues to bring top market prices.

Refiners that handle cheaper crude do so at elevated operating costs. The asphalt portion, incidentally, is used in a number of applications, including road construction. Historically, its use dates back as far as 3,000 years before Christ, when it was used as a building material in Mesopotamia, a fertile area between the Tigris and Euphrates rivers in a country today known as Iraq.)

At Gulf, William Mellon, the nephew of Pittsburgh bankers Andrew and Richard Mellon, decided that the only possible way out of the problem was to build a 450-mile pipeline linking the refinery to the Glenn Pool. His counterpart at Texaco, "Buckskin" Joe Cullinan, came to the same conclusion.

The ramification of those two decisions, made separately and announced weeks apart, was enormous, but incalculable at the time.

Before deciding to build its pipeline, Gulf Refining operated

D. W. Franchot built the first natural gas processing plant west of the Mississippi in the Glenn Pool. His tank cars here are carrying natural gasoline from the field.

in tandem with Guffey Petroleum, which had developed the Spindletop. After the decision, Gulf boldly set sail on its own in an all-or-nothing venture that developed into a fully integrated oil company, with facilities ranging from its wells to service-station gas pumps. It marked a new strategy, one that would be followed by other oil companies.

In advance of its pipeline announcement, Gulf surveyed the field for an extensive gathering system. By late fall of '06, pipeliners were building it, along with a feeder line to Kiefer, where they began constructing a thousand-foot tank-car loading facility, referred to as a rack.

The presence of Gulf-paid pipeliners in the field reportedly prompted Standard Oil agents to warn all the field's operators: Do business with us and us alone or we'll remove our connections to your wells. (This type of practice became illegal in 1909, the second full year of statehood. Pipelines such as those serving the Glenn Pool were required, within reasonable limits, to be non-discriminatory common carriers.)

The growing fight over field domination was expected by all who had done business with Standard. Operating as Prairie Oil and Gas and Prairie Pipeline, it saw big-dollar players coming into the field as intruders and potential threats. For decades, it had established the price for oil by controlling storage, transportation and refineries. But that era was waning; legions of producers and several oil-producing states had cried foul, including Texas, where Standard was kicked out following heated political and legal battles.

Two first-year arrivals into the Glenn Pool, Oklahoma Oil and Associated Producers, were subsidiaries of Tidewater Oil. A group of Pennsylvania producers formed that company in 1879 to build the first long-distance pipeline. Its efficiencies, once the construction cost was paid for, were far greater than rail transportation. But the producers' larger goal was to free themselves from the constraints of Standard. Thus began Standard's long, tireless pursuit of Tidewater. The chase played out in a peculiar way, adversely affecting a Tulsa oil giant, Bill Skelly, while benefiting J. Paul Getty, who would be named the richest man in America in 1957 and recognized publicly as its first billionaire.

By year-end 1906, Standard had built a larger pipeline into the Glenn Pool and was increasing connecting-pipeline capacity to its large refinery in Indiana.

About this same time, a newspaper reported that New York and British financiers planned to build a $20 million pipeline from the field to Dallas and Houston. The man said to be putting this mammoth deal together was Bob Galbreath. Nothing ever came of the proposed pipeline.

A PIG'S EAR AND HARVEY GIRLS

As of the first day in 1907, the *Oil Investors' Journal* reported that the field's 25 operators were daily producing 52,000 barrels, the lion's share being stored in wooden and steel tanks or flowed into pits. One-hundred wells were producing. An honest-to-gosh oil boom was on, spreading as swiftly as the dangerous wildfires.

At the close of January, production had jumped to 64,000 barrels a day from 134 wells. Since development of the field began, drillers had hit only 11 dusters, nearly all outside the proven area. Hitting oil in the Glenn Pool was like shooting ducks on the open

Farmers abandoned their fields, greased their wagon axles, hitched their teams and began hauling equipment to the oil field as teamsters.

oil reservoirs. Thirty-five wells were being drilled simultaneously, and 47 sites were being readied.

The first railcars of crude headed from Kiefer to Texas in February of 1907. Entire trains were dedicated to these shipments, and Gulf's rack was soon expanded to allow loading on both sides, filling 40 tank cars at a time. Several competing loading racks also were built, from within and beyond the field, with Standard Oil centered at Jenks, Texaco at Mounds.

Also in February, work got under way on Gulf's and Texaco's cast-iron, eight-inch pipelines, the industry's largest. And Oklahoma Natural Gas was busy building its gas line west from the field to Oklahoma City.

There were 313 producing wells by the end of April – 413 a month later. During May, Texaco shut in some of its wells because of a lack of tanks, although combined storage for the field had reached four million barrels. At the end of June, 572 wells were producing, and 197 were being drilled.

Wagons loaded with oil equipment formed a ragged line

two miles long from Gulf's off-loading point at Kiefer. Smart-thinking teamsters rolled their wagons on their sides, used the team to lift the freight in place, secured it, righted the

The Tulsa Special, also known as Coal-Oil Johnny, carried workers to and from the Glenn Pool on a dedicated schedule.

wagon, hitched the team back up, and headed for their destination. The work-life of a team was measured not in years but in months; the horses and mules simply wore out from the strain.

Farmers' wives, their husbands often working as teamsters, served up heaping platters of home-cooking for 25 cents. Oil hands, remarking how good it was and thinking the price a bit too much of a bargain, left tips bigger than the price of the meal.

The Mefford family, of Kiefer, set up a 150-foot, three-pole circus tent to serve the hungry men. The clan fed 125 at a time, 300 a day. The head of the household paid the kids two bucks a day. Some of the skilled workers in the field were making five times that or more.

In Tulsa, the Pig's Ear across from the Frisco Depot did, literally, a booming business. The 15-coach oil-field special, dubbed Coal-Oil Johnny, left brimming with passengers bound for the Glenn Pool. On their laps were wrinkled paper sacks of lunch made by Bert Center's wife. They returned hungry at day's end, just in time to watch Bert pull fried chicken from the bubbling, hog-fat grease in the cast-iron skillets. No one was counting cholesterol; no one knew what it was.

If an oil worker could afford it – and if he was cleaned up and attired properly – the place to eat was the Harvey House, nestled in the Frisco's new and elaborate passenger station in Sapulpa. The "Harvey Girls" – young, pretty waitresses in starched brown-and-white uniforms – warned the boys not to cuss; it wasn't allowed. Some of the girls married men from the Glenn Pool, but more hitched their marital stars to railroad workers, who were more likely to stick in one place than roughnecks, roustabouts and the like.

The Midland Valley built a spur from Jenks to Poag, Watkins, and a new place named *Sapulpa's Frisco passenger depot and its upscale Harvey House restaurant.* Glenpool Station. Attempts to extend rail lines more deeply into the field failed after oil operators demanded that loading facilities be included before they allowed the railroads to pass through their leases.

The town of Glenpool emerged as a relatively tranquil and good place to live, in part because no saloons were allowed. Drinking holes also were banned in Sapulpa, although unmarked suitcases crammed with whiskey "mysteriously" appeared at the Frisco Depot and disappeared just as quickly.

Banker-investor Bates Burnett and oilman F. M. Selby, a

transplanted Ohioan, spearheaded construction of an electric rail line into the field from Sapulpa, which they tirelessly supported.

Down at Mounds, a fellow by the name of "Two-Gun" Ike Roller kept the peace. No one was sure whether he was bravely foolish or foolishly brave, but few messed with him more than once.

Tulsa would pave streets, put up street signs and string electric lights. Kiefer, that wild and crazy place, would show its softer side by constructing an opera house, an ice-cream parlor, a library, and a pair of movie houses – plus banks and strings of businesses supporting the field. Preachers and teachers came; churches and a school were built. The town's violence continued unabated, however, and women such as "Two-Ton Tilly" carried on their age-old trade.

Picture postcards spread the field's images internationally. Some showed the earthen pits of crude, causing people unfamiliar with oil fields to believe that Oklahoma was literally bubbling over with lakes of oil. Pictures of massive tank fires also were postcard favorites.

One of the postcards was overprinted with the words, *Oil Field Scene – Tulsa, I.T.* (Indian Territory). An apparent Glenn Pool worker mailed one with the message, "Didn't know I was in Tulsa, did you? Write later."

"For many, postcards were how they learned of oil in Oklahoma. Also, postcards were kept and shared time and time again," says Jim Kemm, past president of the Oklahoma Historical Society and author of *Tulsa, Oil Capital of the World.*

The January 1, 1907, publication of the *Oil Investors' Journal* listed the following as operators in the Glenn Pool: Galbreath,

Associated Producers, Creek Oil, W. H. Milliken, E. J. Bonaker, Quaker Oil, Prairie Oil and Gas, Shawnee Oil, Litchfield and Sawyer, Selby Oil, Laurel Oil, Hoffman, Hall and Reese, Beacon Oil, Chapman and Gooch, Eastern Oil, Oklahoma Oil, Pawnee-Tulsa, Savoy Oil, Commercial Oil, New York Oil, National Oil and Development, Booth Oil, Engelbach Oil, Priest and Preston, and Charles Page. Another source, *The History of Tulsa, a City with a Personality,* identified key early developers of the field, in addition to those above, as: W. H. Roeser, John Mitchell, F. A. Gillespie, J. R. Gillespie, Dr. L. S. Skelton, Robert McFarlin, Harry Sinclair, Harry Rogers, and Oscar Howard. The trouble with such lists is that they often leave out someone.

This picture postcard depicts an oil well coming in.

This postcard misidentifies the Glenn Pool as the Tulsa Oil Field. That's crude oil, not water, in the foreground.

RECORDS AND STATEHOOD

As the intensely hot, drought-ridden, fire-plagued summer of 1907 mercifully approached an end, the field was busier than a three-legged cat in a litter box. Machine shops, repairing, building and sometimes inventing whatever it took to keep things humming in the field, were open 20 hours a day, sometimes around the clock. Supply houses did business in the tens of thousands of dollars every month. Combined storage-tank capacity had climbed to 10 million barrels, testifying to the vast sums of money and labor invested in that area alone.

By the close of August, the production-well count hit 715, including the 97 new arrivals – more than three a day. Eighty-six more wells were being drilled. Grimy, oil-stained bib overalls hanging from the rig indicated that the drilling on that well was finished. The driller, wearing his new pair of overalls and cotton shirt, headed to the next drill site. The bib overalls set him back 75 cents, the cotton shirt, a quarter.

Despite all the new drilling, however, production was declining, particularly in the early wells. The damaging results of "flush production" from the tightly spaced wells was clearly show-ing – just as it had at Spindletop.

(Oil Investors' Journal data point this out: As August opened, some 618 wells were producing an estimated 117,540 barrels daily, a number that equaled the field's best and would stand as the record. Although 97 additional wells came on stream during the month, production decreased by approximately 17,000 barrels. This more-wells, less-production scenario continued. Some volun-tary attempts were made early in 1908 to regulate – diminish – the

Glenn Pool's production but were largely unsuccessful. A quarter-century would pass before sweeping production regulations, led by oilman-turned-Governor E. W. Marland, were in place for Oklahoma and the Mid-Continent region. Designed to protect oil prices and preserve the life of the fields, the action meant that a well might be allowed to produce only a fraction of its capability. This allocation process is known in the industry as "prorationing." On December 7, 1941, the day Pearl Harbor was attacked, the first potent regulation teeth for the Oklahoma Corporation Commission were bared.)

In addition to the excitement generated by the Glenn Pool, another drama was unfolding in the Twin Territories, which had been wrangling over the prospects of statehood since shortly after the Land Run of 1889. No fewer than 10 conventions had been held over the years, with the last one finally resulting in a constitution in April of 1907.

The document was so long it took 18 hours to read. Democrats supported it; Republicans, at the urging of President Teddy Roosevelt, opposed it; and voters approved it, 180,333 to 73,059. On November 16, Oklahoma became the forty-sixth state, with 75 counties; a couple of more were added later.

It could be argued – and some have – that the Glenn Pool hastened statehood. Certainly, little time was wasted in forming the Corporation Commission or in assessing taxes. Benefiting enormously were the school districts in and near the field. Their facilities were often described as the best in the state; some claimed they were as good as any in the nation.

During the initial month of statehood, Glenn Pool oil dropped a nickel a barrel, down to 35 cents. Some 250 tankies were put out of work, marking the first substantial layoffs in the field. Published reports have linked their dismissal to the price drop, but there proba-

Laying the Gulf and Texaco pipelines to the Glenn Pool was grueling work involving thousands of men.

bly was another reason: Total tank storage capacity approached 14 million barrels; the tankies' major work had been accomplished.

By several measures – wells drilled, infrastructure built, pipelines completed or nearing completion, additional companies entering the field – 1907 was the Glenn Pool's greatest year.

When figures were tallied early in January of 1908, some 95 companies were operating in the field, and 1,196 wells were producing. Remarkably, only 15 dry holes were reported. Total production, as reported by the *Oil Investors' Journal*, had topped 27 million barrels. The *Journal* also reported that $15 million had thus far been spent on steel and wood, $5 million for leases, $4.5 million on drilling and well completions, and $3 million for labor. This equates in today's currency to more than half-a-billion dollars spent in the field, whose footprint had expanded to four miles in length, north to south, and more than two miles wide, or roughly 5,000 acres.

(Providing accurate production figures for the very early life

of the field is, at best, difficult. For one thing, all oil production figures in Indian Territory had been lumped in with those of Kansas.
Oklahoma Geological Survey data indicate that slightly more oil
was produced in 1908 than the previous year. Given the continuing
more-wells, less-production scenario, this appears to be debatable.
Also, production figures in those early years were as much guessti-
mates as solid estimates. Modern gauging techniques, involving factors such as temperature and atmospheric pressure; other technology; and uniform reporting methods were yet to come. There also is
this incalculable factor: Under-reporting and over-reporting production held the potential of financial benefit, depending on the cir-
cumstances, for someone so inclined.)

Gulf, in direct competition with Standard, was sending out
Glenn Pool crude on its new pipeline. The line's completion in
October of 1907 had represented an accomplishment of herculean
effort involving several thousand men working south from one end,
north from the other, and in either direction from the middle.
Texaco's pipeline would be completed early in 1908, ending at its
tank farm just south of Tulsa.

The mere announcements that these pipelines would be
built had enticed additional oil companies and money-men into the
Glenn Pool. Gulf sent Frank Loevy to buy as many good, existing
leases as he could. The Gulf subsidiary, Gypsy, named for Loevy's
boat, became one of the larger players in the field. As he and other
deep pockets roamed the field and hotel lobbies, some early
investors sold out, with amazing profit margins.

R. A. Josey plunked down $500 and $600 in separate ventures in 1906. He sold these interests for $150,000 in February of
1907, the month construction began on both pipelines. Other early

Before and during the Glenn Pool oil boom, Sapulpa was a fearsome rival to Tulsa.

investors made far more. It came down to knowing when to hold 'em and when to fold 'em. For example, the field's discoverer reportedly turned down $1.6 million for his leases and wells but later sold out for less than half that.

Gulf and Texaco had spent millions constructing their pipelines and pump stations, but reaped fortunes, not only from the flow of the high-quality Glenn Pool crude purchased at bargain-basement prices, but later from a growing and long-lived presence in Oklahoma. The two interstate pipelines, along with Standard's, played an important role in legitimatizing and empowering Oklahoma as a top-tier player in the oil industry and set the stage for this to continue as boom after boom followed the Glenn Pool's glory days. Cushing, the first to

Sapulpa's claim as The Oil City of the Southwest *was topped by Tulsa's own:* Oil Capital of the World.

boom after the Glenn Pool, would become known as the *Pipeline Crossroads of the World*. A map of these lines resembles spaghetti strands converging on a big platter.

SETTLING THE CONTEST

Tulsa's Commercial Club members became even more excited and boastful – if that were possible – during the boom. They set out on a second national outing in 1908, this time with something to actually brag about. The rail tour carried them nearly 3,000 miles across 15 states in a scant 16 days. In place of Will Rogers, their main attraction was Emmett Dalton, the lone survivor of the bank-robbing Dalton Gang, recently pardoned after serving 14 years in a Kansas prison.

New York Governor Charles Hughes turned out to meet them at Manhattan's Union Station, and they were paraded down Fifth Avenue. President Teddy Roosevelt threw a party for the entire bunch in Washington, where they visited the House and Senate. And when they returned to the Chicago Mercantile Exchange on their trip back home, their antics caused trading by telegraph to be halted until a sense of order resumed.

To anyone who would listen, the boosters claimed that the population of Tulsa would reach 100,000 by 1920. As it turned out, their forecast was nearly three-fourths accurate, a high-water mark of accuracy for the boosters. A crowd estimated at 8,500, much of the town, greeted their jubilant return. Two years later, in 1910, some 18,000 called Tulsa their home. In 1916, its ever-thickening telephone directory listed 431 oil and gas companies.

In a sense, the outcome of the Tulsa-versus-Sapulpa rivalry

Tulsans claimed the Glenn Pool as their own and opened their arms to oilmen and their families, transforming the cow town into a place of promise and prosperity. Here, streets had yet to be paved.

was evident before it was settled. Sapulpa had erected a large, electric sign at the edge of town: *The Oil City of the Southwest.* It was a neat sign, complete with a series of little lights resembling flickering gas flames. Tulsa, about the same time the Commercial Club boys went on their second tour, started referring to itself as the *Oil Capital of the World.* Tulsa also would be described as *The Magic City,* the northeastern Oklahoma area as *The Magic Empire,* with signs saying so on everything that didn't move and some things that did.

Kathryn Hall Dunn, born in Tulsa in 1885, recalled that she grew up believing the city *was* magic. And maybe it was.

"When I was a small girl, we often visited my mother's family in Oklahoma City. I can vividly remember bragging to my cousins there, 'I live in Tulsa – *The Magic City,*' and recall that they were wide-eyed and, I thought, properly impressed, giving me a definite feeling of superiority." (*Tulsa's Magic Roots* by Nina Lane Dunn, Kathryn's daughter-in-law.)

In 1908, the *Oil Investors' Journal* confirmed what everyone else already knew: Tulsa was the center of the oil activity. Based in Beaumont, it had set up a branch office in Tulsa by then. Two years later, the publication was sold for $20,000, its press and barrels of ink were moved to Tulsa, and it was renamed the *Oil & Gas Journal*. It would become known and respected internationally as the "oil man's bible" and the "big yellow book."(The *Journal* is still printed in Tulsa, but its editorial offices are in Houston.)

"We were closer to the oil field, but they were a little more aggressive," says Doris R. Yocham, president of the Sapulpa Historical Society. "Perhaps we didn't know how to deal with them on that level."

Lingering resentment?

"I don't see that. Let Tulsa have the traffic – we like our small town," says the amiable and outgoing Yocham, who worked in Gulf's production office in the Glenn Pool until it closed in 1955.

That same year, during the fiftieth-anniversary celebration of the Ida Glenn, radio broadcaster Glenn Condon remarked, "Why did one oil field do so much for a city? It's a thrilling story. But the story is not so much what the Glenn Pool did *for* Tulsa as a story of what Tulsa did *with* the Glenn Pool." Basically, it opened its arms to the budding industry, with hotels, office buildings, homes and arguably the world's first bank established by oilmen for oilmen, the Exchange National. Condon acknowledged this in his speech, but he said the city's victory ultimately came down to "Tulsa spirit." (The anniversary speech was written by Henry Ralph, of the Chamber of Commerce's Oil Activities Department.)

REVOLUTIONS

Oklahoma became recognized as the nation's number-one oil producing state as the Standard, Gulf and Texaco pipelines pumped 18.5 million barrels of Glenn Pool crude to their refineries in 1908. Another pipeline, Sinclair, would be built, bringing oil to its refinery at Coffeyville, Kansas, and, in 1918, on to the Great Lakes region.

Although oil in pipelines moves slowly — about the pace of a brisk walk — its flow is uniquely continuous and far more efficient and safer than any other transportation method. But why not build a refinery in Tulsa and virtually eliminate the field-to-refinery transportation costs?

Tulsa's Commercial Club members had just that idea as early as 1906, when the Glenn Pool was beginning to flex its muscles. Unfortunately, they pursued the notion.

They provided a 15-acre site, situated on the west side of the Arkansas River not far from downtown, and solicited investors to build the Uncle Sam Refinery, a little 600-barrel-a-day unit.

The *Tulsa World* opposed the entire promotion, while the *Tulsa Democrat* rooted for it. In the end, no one felt like saluting Uncle Sam. Author Bob Gregory wrote in 1980: *The World was right all the way – the Uncle Sam Refinery went bust, its president bankrupt and under indictment.*

The Sapulpa Oil Refinery was built in 1907, changed hands several times, and was moved to Ponca City in 1928 as a part of Continental Oil. Texaco built a large refinery in 1910 at its tank-farm and rail-shipping point two miles south of Tulsa. The Sinclair Refinery operates there today.

About three years later, a man who had overcome a series of hard-luck experiences at Bigheart – renamed Barnsdall — built another large refinery, this one about where the ill-fated Uncle Sam had been. Josh Cosden's Mid-Continent refinery and his beautiful office building by the same name made an indelible imprint on Tulsa, but he would die broke. (See *Characters and Kind Hearts.*) The refinery, through many changes and iterations, is now Sunoco.

The Glenn Pool's overall production remained fairly steady from 1908 through 1910, according to Oklahoma Geological Survey figures. This feat was accomplished by the development of the Taneha Extension, near Sapulpa; some new drilling in the original field; and the cleaning, shooting, and occasional deeper drilling of existing wells.

During 1912, the Glenn Pool's total production eclipsed the 100-million-barrel mark, forever identifying it as one of America's major oil fields. Production that year came in at just under 10.5 million barrels and would continue to diminish. New drilling had decreased dramatically. Fewer bib overalls hung on the rigs.

Also in 1912, the Standard Oil Trust responded to high-court rulings by breaking itself into what became known as the "Seven Sisters." Over time, the largest Sister, Standard Oil of New Jersey, became Exxon. In addition to the Seven Sisters, at least 24 other Standard Oil companies were involved in the court-mandated breakup. But if the John Rockefeller critics and haters thought the dismantling would hurt him, they were wrong – he became richer still. In relative terms, Rockefeller was richer during his era than Microsoft Chairman Bill Gates, listed by Forbes magazine in

John D. Rockefeller

2005 as the wealthiest man in the world.

Millions of Model T Fords and other automobiles were coughing through cities, towns and the countryside, the revolutions of their internal-combustion engines creating a revolution in the oil industry. In only the third year of the Model T's production, 1910, gasoline had become the primary product, displacing kerosene.

Glenn Pool operators had anticipated higher prices ever since the first competing interstate pipeline came to their field. But the higher prices never came, at least not during the field's peak performance. When the Cushing Field was discovered in 1912, oil prices had reached 76 cents a barrel, soon climbing past a dollar. The Cushing Field physically was several times larger than the Glenn Pool. In 1914, it

Model T Ford production alone strongly influenced the nation's demand for gasoline. For a number of years, half of all the U.S. cars manufactured were Model Ts.

pushed past the 300,000-barrel-a-day mark, nearly three times the Glenn Pool's best of 117,500. Overall, the Glenn Pool and the Cushing Field have produced north of 330 million barrels and half-a-billion barrels, respectively.

Some oilmen, Bob Galbreath among them, have said that figures-only comparisons of these two major oil fields fail to tell the whole story.

Galbreath said, "Comparing the Glenn Pool with the Cushing Field, I believe the former should be given credit for being the greatest oil field in Oklahoma for this reason: The Glenn Pool was developed on an average-price oil of 30 cents, with lack of pipelines and other facilities contributing to the development and profit of an oil property. When the Cushing Field was discovered, conditions were entirely different. The price of oil had reached one dollar, and the pipelines were ready to take the production.

The boom town of Cushing arose after Tom Slick discovered the Cushing Field in 1912, when Glenn Pool production was half that of its best years.

Oklahoma was then under state government, and whole reams of red tape (that) retarded the taking of leases in early Glenn Pool days had been torn away, and a legitimate operator could secure a lease and feel reasonably sure of holding it in the Cushing Field." (*The History of Tulsa, Oklahoma, a City with a Personality*)

The age of energy – oil energy – was making itself known with each passing year. Revolutionary technology that converted refineries from overgrown distilleries to something called fractionators, thermally cracking the molecules into precise fractions resulting in more and better products; massive conversions from coal to fuel oil, including Winston Churchill's brave decision to convert the British Navy; the demands of World War I; vastly increasing numbers of autos, planes, tractors, and new machinery – all these and more contributed heavily to the historic transformation and, in ways that continue to change the world, a growing dependence on crude.

Oklahoma repeatedly would take the spotlight as the nation's number-one producing state and remain a top-tier player for decades, its first mighty push coming from a piece of land no more than nine miles long and a few miles wide named for a farmer and his wife who had received a 160-acre allotment in a strange payment relating to the forced march of her ancestors into a place the government thought was pretty much worthless and undesirable.

A quarter of a century ago, Kenny Franks, author of *The Oklahoma Oil Industry,* summed up the big-picture significance of the field named for Bob and Ida Glenn as well as anyone ever has:

The impact of Glenn Pool lived far beyond the heyday of the field. It was Glenn Pool that brought the pipelines to Oklahoma and opened new marketing outlets. It was Glenn Pool that caused the great influx of capital into

Oklahoma that would make continued development of the industry possible. And it was Glenn Pool that focused the eyes of the nation on the petroleum industry in Oklahoma.

This illustration depicts Tulsa in its heyday as the bona fide Oil Capital of the World. *The Mid-Continent refinery, built by Josh Cosden and originally known as the Cosden refinery, is in the foreground.*

Chapman   McFarlin

FROM THE GLENN POOL

CHARACTERS AND KIND HEARTS

here is a legend in the oil fields that some men are approached early in life by a bird made of cast iron, whose voice is found in the hoarse squawk of a walking beam in need of oil, in the shriek of a wild plume of black oil tearing from the ground into the freedom of the sky, and in the hissing roar of a wild gas fire, lighting up the earth like a tremendous red torch. Once a man has been visited by the Dicky Bird, he will never find rest until he has cast all else aside and plunged into the feverish search for oil, wherever it may lead him.

The colorful description appears in the opening of Bob Duncan's book, *The Dicky Bird Was Singing*, published more than half a century ago. During the Glenn Pool's powerhouse years leading to the next major oil boom, the *Dicky Bird* screamed. Some oilmen tamed the bird, riding it to heights unimaginable, exiting with grace and lasting generosity. Others, intoxicated by the flight, crashed upon the shoals of life. And one – teased, mocked and eventually honored by rich and poor alike – stood apart from them all.

Each person who entered Oklahoma's first major oil field left with a story worth telling. The following vignettes portray a few of these characters and kind hearts.

'Oklahoma's Mystery Millionaire'

Independent oil producer Eddie Rongey, a third-generation veteran of the Glenn Pool, had advised that the field still holds secrets and mysteries. Or as he candidly observed, "If anyone tells you they know everything there is to be known about these wells or this field, they are really stupid or they're lying."

One of the Glenn Pool's many unanswered questions revealed itself not in the field, however, but on page 15 of a book: *The McMan, The Lives of Robert M. McFarlin and James A. Chapman.*

Authors Carl Tyson, James Thomas and Odie Faulk wrote that McFarlin mortgaged his house at Holdenville for $800 to buy 40 acres near Kiefer. That in itself is unremarkable, but the year of the purchase certainly is – 1903. Although oilmen and speculators were nosing around the area even before then, the discovery of the

Robert McFarlin

oil field was still two years into the foggy future.

As recently as 2005, a spokesperson familiar with McFarlin said that he "leased" the 40 acres near Kiefer before the Glenn Pool discovery. But regardless of whether the land was bought or leased, the question goes begging – why?

If the land were bought, it is likely that it came from a freedman; Creek Indians weren't allowed to sell their land allotments at the time. If it were leased for drilling purposes, the Interior Department's Office of Indian Affairs would have required this to occur far sooner than the two-plus years that transpired before McFarlin had his first rig in the Glenn Pool.

Now, why would a rancher-farmer who had never before looked for oil hock his two-story home to buy a patch of pasture some 70 miles northeast of his cattle operations? To borrow on something out of the Watergate era, and meaning no disrespect to McFarlin, *What did he know and when did he know it?*

There apparently is no good and ready answer to the question, and therein lies the mystery.

A family-and-friend partnership brand new to oil drilled on the 40-acre tract at Kiefer in 1906, the first full year of the Glenn Pool's development. The partnership consisted of McFarlin, his nephew James Chapman, Chapman's father, Phillip, and their close friend H. B. Gooch. And they found oil – lots of oil.

McFarlin and James Chapman weren't interested in wildcatting. Spending money on anything so uncertain wasn't in their nature. Their business sense demanded that they stand back, wait for oil to be found, and then march in with money, men, and equipment for their share of the field.

Some oilmen in the Glenn Pool saw the heavy sheets of oil

resting atop the flowing creek waters – and nothing more. Chapman saw money. He pulled booms onto the creek, corralled the oil, siphoned it off, and hauled it back to waiting storage tanks owned by the partners. The simple but overlooked conservation method provided them with a nearly no-expense return involving little more than sweat and labor.

Before the close of 1907, when Gooch sold his interest to the other three, the partners were richer than they could have dreamed of becoming as farmers and ranchers in Holdenville or their native Texas.

The all-family operation became even more tightly knitted in 1908 when Chapman married Leta, the older daughter of Robert and Ida McFarlin. Key to the foursome's makeup was a purpose-driven life, differing only marginally by religious preferences – the McFarlins being Methodists, the Chapmans, Presbyterians. Individually and collectively, the McFarlins and Chapmans proved to be models of philanthropy, providing critical funding for education, health care and religion, not only in Tulsa, where they finally settled after the men commuted for years back and forth from Holdenville, but elsewhere in Oklahoma, Texas and Arkansas.

After Tom Slick discovered the Cushing Field in March of 1912, McFarlin and Chapman sold all of their Glenn Pool properties, established McMan Oil – the name formed from parts of their names – and were drilling in the new field by August.

Although they had no interest in finding a new field, they seemed to have a sixth sense and extraordinary luck when it came to drilling in proven areas. In the Cushing Field, they didn't like the looks of their first well and pulled up the tools at 600 feet. More poorly

Leta and James Chapman on one of their showplace ranches,
which were measured in the tens of thousands of acres.

financed operators never would have done that. At their second well, they found oil in a formation substantially shallower than that of the discovery well, quickly opening a new area of the field to lower-cost drilling with impressive results. They expanded their operations to the Healdton Field, discovered the same year Slick made his strike, and up into Kansas.

Only four years after entering the Cushing Field, they quietly let it be known that they might sell McMan Oil – if the timing and money were right. It was 1916, and new federal tax laws were scheduled to go into effect on the first day of the new year. Near the end of 1916, McFarlin received a telephoned offer for the company, told the caller that the $39 million amount just mentioned "seemed agreeable," and turned to pass the phone to Chapman.

"Don't want to talk about it any more, Mac," said Chapman, who had overheard the figure. "If it's all right with you, it's all right with me. Tell him we'll take the deal." *(The McMan)*

A Standard Oil entity was the buyer. All but $4 million of the transaction was completed before year-end. At the time, McMan Oil was the largest independent, pure-production company in the nation, with 25,000-barrel yields every day from leases spread across 80,000 acres in Oklahoma and Kansas. The sale established the record paid for a production company, a dollar-mark that stood for several decades. *The Oil & Gas Journal* reported that the four-year-old company had accomplished nothing less than "business miracles." (The McMan stakeholders included McFarlin, James Chapman, Phillip Chapman, and Earl Harwell, as well as Harry Rogers, the company attorney.)

Twenty-one months later, McMan Oil and Gas was formed, operated for 12 years, and was sold in 1930, again to a Standard Oil entity, for $20 million. It was the first full year of the Great Depression. The company probably would have brought far less had it been sold later during that dark period.

Although they shared family values, work ethic and business standards, McFarlin and Chapman were night-and-day different in personality. McFarlin was extremely outgoing and comfortable being at the center of wide-ranging civic and social roles until his health began to fail about 1920. (He lived 22 more years, dying at age 79.) Publicly shy and more comfortable working in the background, Chapman was allergic to cigarette smoke, reporters, and publicity, not necessarily in that order.

The two individually returned to their first love, ranching, their growing spreads being measured in the tens of thousands of acres. Chapman pieced together some of the largest and best-run cattle ranches in the nation, including the Chapman-Barnard Ranch, in Osage County, which at one time totaled 100,000 acres. Again, it was a family business – Horace Barnard was the brother of Chapman's mother-in-law, Ida McFarlin, and had been a stakeholder in the oil business with Chapman, McFarlin and the others.

When Chapman died in 1966 at the age of 80, the *Tulsa World* referred to him as *Oklahoma's mystery millionaire who loved to give money away but hated to get credit for it.* For several decades, he had donated large sums of money based on the stipulation that he would remain anonymous in his lifetime. His fortune at death was estimated at $120 million. It all went into a series of trusts, the embryo of which was established in 1949. When Leta died in 1974, her wealth and his were combined, creating philanthropic trusts valued at $200 million.

By the fiftieth anniversary of the original Chapman trust in 1999, the value had grown to $1.2 billion. During the previous year, the trusts provided $46 million in funding – the equivalent of donating $126,000 every day of the year – to 16 institutions. By early in 2005, the trusts' value had reached $1.4 billion.

The 16 beneficiaries are: the University of Tulsa, Holland Hall School, Hillcrest Medical Center, St. John Health System, Tulsa Area United Way, Tulsa Psychiatric Center, Children's Medical Center, and Saint Simeon's Episcopal Home, all of Tulsa; the Oklahoma Medical Research Foundation and the Episcopal Diocese of Oklahoma, both of Oklahoma City; John Brown

University, of Siloam Springs, Arkansas; Presbyterian Children's Services, of Austin; the Southwest Foundation for Biomedical Research, Saint Mary's Hall, and Trinity University, all of San Antonio; and Southern Methodist University, of Dallas.

Every day, tens of thousands are touched by Oklahoma's largest philanthropic organization. Its catalyst was the Glenn Pool, where a couple of honest, kind-hearted and civic-minded ranchers tried a new line of work a century ago.

'Daddy Page'

Charles Page was 42 years old when he came to Tulsa in 1903 with $25,000 in cash, a medley of adventures, and a long-ago promise yet to be kept.

Big for his age, he had worked in the logging operations of Wisconsin when he was big enough to swing an axe; served as a police chief in a Minnesota town and later as a Pinkerton detective; was a colonization agent for a railroad in the Northwest; lost his shirt trying to corner the prune market; mined for gold in British Columbia and Colorado; bought a hotel and developed affordable housing in Denver; and drilled for oil here and there, finally achieving modest success north of the original Red Fork Field.

By the time of the Glenn Pool discovery, however, his money was almost gone, his only reliable income coming from his hotel in Denver. A promise he had made to his widowed mother as a young boy back in Stevens Point, Wisconsin, however, would set Page apart from all others drawn to the oil field.

After her husband's death, Page's mother had turned their large home into a boarding house, where she washed clothes and cooked meals for the local railroad workers. Charles, the seventh of eight children and not yet 11 years old, helped as best he could by selling pan-ready rabbits for 10 cents apiece. Seeing his mother struggle, he embraced her, promising that someday he would make life better for similarly situated mothers and children.

As a man, Page experienced his own share of grief. He married a widow, Lucille, who had a young son, and planned for a large family. The couple had a baby while he was working in the Pacific Northwest, but the child was stillborn. Lucille, in frail health for years, died in 1906 – the year Page entered the Glenn Pool.

Taught as a boy to be resourceful but not wasteful, he capped the gassers early on when most were flaring them into the sky, bought other gas-well leases inexpensively, and profited as uses and markets expanded for a fuel that once had been seen as a nuisance, its main value seen as its ability to bring tag-along oil to the surface.

Although Page had little formal education, he was an astute businessman, an inventive master at making deals that seemed to satisfy both sides of the bargain. As a lad, he once had traded a whistle for a puppy, and the puppy for a dog sled. He hitched his dog to the sled, slid over the snow-packed roads to the railroad depot, and persuaded the agent to hire him as a messenger after vowing that he would buy a horse with earnings from the job.

His greatest success in the Glenn Pool came in the Taneha Extension, where one of his wells flowed at 2,000 barrels a day. He sold a lease there for a million dollars and extended his oil and gas activities to Osage County and south into Texas. By 1919, after a lengthy and complicated court battle over a valuable lease was resolved in his favor, he was among the richest men in Oklahoma, with extensive real estate holdings in addition to his oil and gas businesses.

But financial success is not the Charles Page story. The real story centers on the promise – neglected, perhaps even forgotten, then pursued with a passion and purpose seldom witnessed.

With its four major railroads, Tulsa was drawing hundreds of people from across the nation every day. The Frisco alone provided three passenger runs from St. Louis and four from Kansas City. The railroad's newspaper advertisements boasted that riders "will travel to the Tulsa Oil Fields in the best time and with the most comfort" on "splendidly equipped trains."

But many weren't arriving in splendid fashion. They came hungry and tired, hunkered in the corners of freight trains loaded with oil-field equipment. Transients, homeless boys, out-of-work fathers, widowed mothers – all were converging on Tulsa.

In response, The Salvation Army sent Captain B. F. Breeding and his family from Kansas to Tulsa in 1907. Breeding and Page quickly became allies, with the oilman spending thousands to provide meals and overnight lodging for hard-luck travelers seeking a ray of hope for a better life.

The next year, Page began buying land seven miles west of Tulsa in a wilderness where clear, wonderfully drinkable spring water bubbled through the purifying sands to the surface. The area and the town, as unique as its founder, would be named Sand Springs.

Soon, Page sent three men to begin clearing a hilly, heavily wooded area. One of them had only one foot, another one good eye, and the third was elderly with a recent drinking past. They started with nothing more than a tent, some tools and supplies, but it was a new beginning. By midsummer, Captain Breeding resigned from The Salvation Army, packed up his family, and joined them on his own 40-acre tract provided by Page. Breeding would devote the rest of his long life to the mission of helping others there.

In 1909, the Cross and Anchor orphans' home near Tulsa was financially failing. Page looked into the situation and was shocked to learn that siblings were being adopted out individually. He wrote a check to prevent the orphanage from going into immediate receivership and told administrators to stop all adoptions unless an only child was involved. A week later, on his birthday, he sent four wagons to pick up beds, furniture, and the 21 boys and girls – the nucleus of what would become the Sand Springs Children's Home.

Charles Page, center, dedicated his life and fortune to helping children and widows. Directly in front of Page is Opal Bennefield Clark, who wrote a book about the philanthropist.

Page had just turned 49. From that point forward, everything he did centered on helping others – orphans, widows, down-and-outers. That same year, he started the Home's first commercial enterprise, selling bottled spring water to Tulsans, and married a former waitress with the same first name as that of his late wife but spelled with only two Ls – Lucile Rayburn.

Cynics, bewildered by the unending trail of men, women and children migrating to the rugged, often swampy land in the middle of nowhere, referred to the undertaking as a "fool's enterprise" and "Page's folly." They spread rumors of ulterior motives that must be driving an otherwise intelligent man to fritter away his fortune. Some felt certain that Page was preparing to run for political office, maybe governor. He never did.

Unlike a number of oilmen who amassed fortunes and later established philanthropies – certainly praiseworthy – Page plunged headfirst into his cause. He paced the floors on sleepless nights, worrying that his cash would not hold up as crude prices dropped or a new well failed.

His stream of fresh ideas constantly outran the manpower – and sometimes the money – to complete the projects at hand. His sweeping vision brought forth a well-planned industrial town with free lots for churches and factories; good water, cheap natural gas, and electricity from a new power plant; a world-class orphanage, the first of which resembled a Southern mansion; a dairy farm and creamery, vegetable gardens, cannery, orchards, and greenhouse; a series of cottages providing rent-free housing for widowed mothers and, for each of their kids, a fresh quart of milk daily; a box factory, cotton gin, flour mill, and brick plant; a lake and amusement park; the Sand Springs Railway, linking people and factories to Tulsa; a school and a hospital; a dam and reservoir on Shell Creek to the west with a 35-inch wooden pipeline bringing the water to Sand Springs and over to Josh Cosden's refinery; the largest cotton mill west of the Mississippi; and on and on.

Page had kept the promise to his mother. Fearing that his luck would change if he took credit for what he believed was God's work, he put his name on nothing – except the checks to keep growing the enterprise.

In 1915, Vernon Whiting of the *Pawhuska Capital* (later the *Pawhuska Journal-Capital*) wrote:

All of the children in the Sand Springs Home have the best there is. The middle of this summer (Page) took a party of 30 of the older children in a special (railroad) car to the Exposition at San Francisco, and gave them a three-week pleasure and sightseeing trip.

Children and staff gather outside the original 1910 Sand Springs Home, which appeared more like a Southern mansion than an orphanage – a word Charles Page shunned.

Each of the children in the Home has an individual bed, and there is no mixing of clothing. He has an athletic director for the boys as well as the girls, and he has a manual trainer for the boys who teaches them wood carving and engraving. He maintains his own school and the teachers for the schools, and on Sundays the school house is used for a church.

For the girls, he maintains two music rooms and teachers. The older children help about the Home – the boys on the farm and the girls at whatever they can do. Page has enough industries that he can provide work for all of the boys of his Home when they may arrive at age, and enough money that he can give both boys and girls an education in whatever line as they may wish to go.

The newspaper reporter added, *Drilling developed the fact that he had oil and gas underneath all of the land he had purchased for his (children's) home. The land was bought for farming land, but it had beneath it a great bed of the driest gas in the entire Mid-Continent Field. Nature was also good in placing beneath the same land at a depth of about 200 feet a great vein of coal running more than three feet thick.*

Later in the same year that Whiting wrote the article, a bashful little girl and several of her siblings came to live in the Home. Vibrant and clear-minded, Opal Bennefield Clark now is 93 years old. Her eyes light up when she is asked if she can remember the moment she met Charles Page.

"It was a Sunday evening," Opal says. "I saw the kids all rushing out the door – Daddy Page was coming! He came almost every evening, and he always took the new ones on his knee. I was shy, but I noticed the sun sparkling on the watch chain looped across his chest. I ventured to touch it. He saw me, took out his watch, and held it up to my ear. I had never seen a watch."

"Do you hear that?" Page softly asked.

"Yes," she meekly replied.

"That's a June bug."

"Can it get out?"

"Oh, that's just a clock," Page reassured, responding to her concern.

She says the Home's matrons and others were "strict but fair. We each had a chore; mine, when I was older, was keeping the little girls' playroom clean. I remember feeling so put-upon, but it was a wonderful life. We were privileged, raised like little rich kids, the best-dressed in town."

The oilman died on December 27, 1926, at age 66. The next day, a Tuesday, *The Tulsa Tribune* wrote: *Charles Page is dead, and today Tulsa, Sand Springs and all the region in between are in shocked mourning ... The great man passed as twilight settled Monday afternoon. He had been ill for a week. A cold and the influenza that followed combined with a diabetic poisoning to slay him ... Exclamations of shocked sorrow and wails of distressed children mingled with the prayers of the multitude.*

The newspaper, which Page had owned before selling it to the son of a preacher, Richard Lloyd Jones, in 1919, noted that Lucile and the couple's adopted daughter, Mary Ann, were at his side when he died. The *Tribune* reassured readers that the Sand Springs Children's Home and Widows' Colony would continue. Page had placed his holdings in a trust dedicated to the Home, reserving only enough to maintain his family and their home.

"Charles Page gave all that he had," Jones said of his close friend.

He pulled a passage from the Bible: *Inasmuch as ye have done it unto the least of these, my brethren, ye have done it unto me.* (The Bible passage appears at the base of a bronze statue of Page, bordered on one side by a widow and her baby, on the other by two orphaned children. The statue is in a triangle immediately south of the former Page Memorial Library, donated to the city of Sand Springs by Lucile after her husband's death.)

The funeral was held Thursday in the expansive living room of the Home. Opal and her sister, Beulah, had hoped to squeeze inside, but couldn't get close. As they and hundreds outside listened to the services on loudspeakers, Beulah urged Opal to form a box-like shape with her arms to provide breathing space from the crushing throng.

The Bennefield sisters were amazed at what they heard.

"We had no idea of all he had done," Opal says. "We didn't even know what he did for a living or how he made his money. To us, he was just Daddy Page. I turned to my sister and whispered, 'Someday I am going to write a book about him.'"

(She did. *A Fool's Enterprise*, a love-filled tribute, was first published in 1988 and is available in its fourth edition. Details for this sketch on the oilman largely came from her book. Opal has since written and illustrated a children's book and now is writing of her life as a Home girl — one of the very few surviving who personally knew Page.)

At the Page mansion in Oklahoma's first and only planned industrial town, a wolf-like dog pensively waited at the foot of his master's chair. "Jim" heard the church bells toll and the industry sirens sing that day. For 17 years, the canine served as Charles Page's faithful advisor, his actions signaling whether each person who approached — there were literally thousands — was of good heart or up to no good.

"In a real sense, Jim was Mr. Page's business partner," says Ruth Ellen Henry, programs and public information director at the Sand Springs Museum, the former Page Memorial Library. "If Jim's fur ruffled or he turned his back, it was a signal that they weren't trustworthy. If his tail wagged and he took up with them, they got just about everything they asked for."

When his master died, Jim refused to eat, his eyes dimmed, and he, too, died.

"He grieved himself to death," says Ruth Ellen.

A song, written by a private-school teacher identified as Mrs. Wiggins, for years was sung to the philanthropist by children at the Home. It asks:

What would you take for me Daddy Page,
If someone wanted to buy,
And stacked all the bright shiny dollars
In a pile up as high as the sky.

Opal Bennefield Clark wrote that Charles Page, upon hearing the children sing the song, wiped tears from his eyes.

"There aren't enough dollars in the world to buy you," he replied.

(Twenty-eight kids were being cared for by the Sand Springs Children's Home early in 2005. Each has the promise of a free college education, among other benefits. Several thousand children have graduated from the Home. Many have become doctors, attorneys, teachers and business leaders. Widowed mothers with two or more children continue to reside close by in Page Villages, originally known as the Widows' Colony. A quart of milk continues to be delivered daily for each of the children.)

Riding High, Crashing Hard

As a part of a teaching-support program by the Oklahoma Energy Resources Board, high school students are being asked what they would do with $10 million. The ghost of Billy Roeser would reply: "Better make that fifty million. No, wait; I'll need more than that." ·

No one rode the *Dicky Bird* with more flair or crashed it harder than this dapper, carefree and likeable spendthrift. Born to an oil family in Marietta, Ohio, he came full circle in the Glenn Pool, entering the field nearly broke and returning to it years later the same way. In between, he spent millions on a sky-high lifestyle.

Before entering the Glenn Pool, he had tried his oil luck in Texas, as well as at Muskogee and Cleveland in Indian Territory. Soon, he was operating three companies in the Glenn Pool and netting an estimated $3,000 a day – the equivalent of nearly $60,000 in today's dollars. But that was only the beginning.

Author Bob Gregory described the inimitable oilman this way in a special edition magazine by the Tulsa Chamber of Commerce on the field's seventy-fifth anniversary:

Billy was well-liked by people who saw in him a gift for laughing at what life is supposed to mean. He loved to spend, not save; he loved to drink, drive recklessly and thumb his nose at anyone who sought to pass judgment. Roeser didn't care what people thought, only about what he did. And the only person he ever mistreated was himself.

When Billy got rolling, he bought the biggest, most impressive house in Tulsa – George Bayne's place at 1437 South Boulder – for $35,000. That he had never seen inside the house didn't matter. When he did see it, he ordered everything out – chairs, tables, rugs, paintings, dishes. Most of it was claimed by friends. He redecorated for $65,000. He knew nothing of art, so he told a

Billy Roeser in one of his many new automobiles. The young passenger is Roeser's daughter, Ruth.

dealer, *"You send me $16,000 worth of real, genuine oil paintings."*

Gregory wrote that Roeser had bluegrass sod railed in from Missouri at a cost of $7,000 and spent another $8,500 for trees and shrubs.

He added that Roeser *hired a Kansas City caterer, his chef, waiters, dishes and an orchestra; down they came for $5,000. Billy also gave $5,000 to a church and thousands to his friends. He would buy six cars at a time – $14,000 – and then give them away.*

When one of his cars became hopelessly stuck in the mud, Billy sold it for $200. It was easier to buy a new one.

He never stopped looking for oil. Toward the end, he leased 110,000 acres in Illinois but came away with nothing. Good fortune had become a familiar stranger to Billy Roeser. When his luck and his money finally played out, he sold everything. His paintings and furnishings wound up in the homes of more fortunate oilmen. The expensive china and a beautiful table went into service at the Sand Springs Children's Home, where the kids had no idea of their value. Some friends loaned him enough money to have another go at it, and he drilled that away. According to some reports, he returned one last time to where he had become rich, the Glenn Pool, but it no longer held anything for him.

It was reported that he blew through $50 million – incredible if true, for that figure would translate to the south side of a billion today. He looked upon it all with nonchalance. After all, he reasoned, he was no poorer than when he began chasing the *Dicky Bird*. And, oh, what a breathtaking flight it had been.

Such stories of making it and losing it were common, differing only in time, scale and detail.

THE MASTER

His balding head was oversized for his body, perhaps because of the unusually large cerebral matter it contained. His broadly set blue eyes pierced those wishing his attention, going beyond their countenance and into their souls. Over the years, his lips turned down at the edges, forming a permanent frown that only added to the image and aura of power, described by some as Napoleonic.

People in his boyhood home in Independence, Kansas, originally thought that he didn't have a good head, large as it was, for business. Later, others who didn't actually know Harry Sinclair, and those who didn't like him, said he built the giant oil company bearing his name by being lucky. They were wrong – he was incredibly shrewd and savvy.

Sinclair wanted to be bigger than John D. Rockefeller, and

gave it a real shot, creating one of the largest petroleum companies in the land. His joy at finding oil – he once had 40 wildcats operating simultaneously – was surpassed by his delight in crafting deals. In his view, oil properties were meant to be sold, at the right price, so larger, more promising properties could be bought. He had the unusual ability to make buyers and sellers alike feel as though he was doing them a favor by doing business with them, like a king dealing with his subjects.

Born in West Virginia in 1876, he wound up in the southeastern Kansas town of Independence, where his father established a drug store. It looked as if Harry would follow in his footsteps. He studied at the University of Kansas and returned home to run the store, but lost the business – some said to a speculative deal that failed – before he was 21.

The story has been told and retold how the young man accidentally shot off one of his toes while hunting rabbits. The toe was amputated, and Harry collected $5,000 from an insurance policy. His critics put a different twist on the story, implying that the discharge might not have been accidental. For those who dared ask, Sinclair replied only that it made for a good yarn.

The money was put to use buying and selling timbers used as foundations for derricks popping up in southeastern Kansas. From those profits, he

Harry Sinclair

bought oil leases and hired drilling contractors. One of those, W. L. Connelly, presented his bill, struck up a conversation, and was invited to use a desk in Sinclair's three-room workplace above the Independence Post Office.

In addition to drilling wells, Connelly began scouting potential leases for Sinclair. He worked for about four months without pay before checking with Sinclair to make sure he actually was employed.

"Sure," Sinclair replied. "Why do you ask that question?"

His bank account nearly depleted, Connelly explained that he hadn't been compensated. They agreed on a salary, the office manager filled in a check, and a relationship that would last half a century was formed. The small-framed oilman rose to chairman of the board at Sinclair Oil. He wrote of his and Sinclair's worldwide adventures in *The Oil Business as I saw It*, published in 1954.

Connelly described his boss as "the only one of his model," a man who "never wheedled or coddled. He gave orders and expected them to be executed, but when he gave his friendship it stuck as long as it was deserved." Connelly thought so much of him that he and his wife named their son Harry Sinclair.

Sinclair was fairly well heeled when he entered the Glenn Pool, having already pocketed more than $100,000, including substantial revenues from the Kiowa Field in 1905.

Ruth Sheldon Knowles, author of *The Greatest Gamblers*, wrote: *When he heard of a new strike on the Ida Glenn farm near Tulsa, Sinclair went there so quickly that he was able to buy some of the choicest leases before prices rocketed beyond the reach of his budding new bank account.*

The Glenn Pool made him rich. Like other independent operators, Sinclair faced the dilemma of low prices for his crude, but he had the money to store it and wait for better times or buyers; he didn't care which. His brain whirled, with leases being bought, swapped and sold like properties on a Monopoly board – always with the intent of controlling the game. His success was influenced by the fact that Connelly proved to be an astute and nearly inexhaustible scout.

When a rifle-toting farmer wouldn't allow Connelly to move a rig through his land to a new lease in the Glenn Pool, he went to Sapulpa, explained the situation to a Creek Indian policeman, and persuaded him to accompany him and the rig past the angry man.

Back in Independence, Sinclair asked Connelly why he hadn't just ignored the farmer in the first place.

"Well," Connelly replied, "that rifle looked a lot bigger when it was shoved into my anatomy than it could look from the office here in Independence, one hundred miles away."

Sinclair sent Connelly everywhere, with precious little notice or explanation. When a Texas Panhandle businessman told Sinclair he had gas flowing somewhere under his store – a haberdashery he had converted from a restaurant – Connelly traveled to Dalhart in the middle of a blizzard. It didn't take Connelly long to figure that the gas "find" was originating from a cesspool loaded with kitchen grease. He headed back through the storm to Independence and new assignments from the boss.

Bankers in the early Glenn Pool years, attuned to the needs of farmers, ranchers and merchants, were as comfortable with the oil business as a drunk in church. This changed in 1910 when Sinclair and other wealthy oilmen – Patrick White, J. H. Evans, F. B. Ufer, Robert McFarlin and James Chapman – established the

Exchange National Bank in Tulsa. Arguably the world's first true oil bank, it understood oilmen's risks and needs, and welcomed their business. As fields were developed by Tulsa-connected oil companies, money flowed into the bank from as near as Oklahoma and as far as South America and the Middle East.

(The Exchange National was rescued by Sinclair, Chapman and others in the Great Depression and reorganized as the National Bank of Tulsa, later the Bank of Oklahoma. The Bank of Oklahoma Tower, also referred to as the Williams Tower, is the tallest – 52 stories – and the last of the downtown skyscrapers. It was completed in 1977 as the new headquarters for The Williams Companies, whose founders came to Tulsa in 1916 to build cross-country oil and gas pipelines.)

Most of the oil deals, however, didn't originate in Tulsa's banks. They were made at the backs of wagons, on oil-slick derrick floors, and in hotel lobbies. When the opulent, 12-story Hotel Tulsa was completed in the spring of 1912, the *Tulsa World* hailed it as yet "another milestone in the onward march" of the city. The hotel immediately became a magnet for oil-field scuttlebutt and deals.

W. N. Robinson, whose hotel in earlier years had drawn ire over its sewage problems, strolled over to run the plush Hotel Tulsa. Taking note of the hotel's role as mecca for oilmen, Robinson declared that "no well drilled in the lobby shall stop at any shallow sands; every well must go down to the deep pay and represent an outlay of at least ten-thousand dollars. The woods are full of posthole diggers – we are after the deep production."

In the hotel's marble-floored, dome-ceilinged lobby, million-dollar checks were written more times than could be recorded by the oil reporters, who spent as much time there as in their news-rooms. *Democrat* and later *Tribune* reporter Rosella Flanagan set up her desk in a corner of the lobby, where Josh Cosden inked a $12 million check for the purchase of Hill Oil & Gas. By one estimate, more than a billion dollars in deals transpired at Hotel Tulsa before it was supplanted by the larger, more modern Mayo Hotel in the mid '20s.

Sinclair looked upon the constant lobby goings-on with the amusement of an adult watching kids at play. While still commuting by train from Independence, he leased a suite of offices on the fifth floor and

Some of the biggest oil deals in the world were routinely struck in the Hotel Tulsa (inset), which opened in 1912. The larger, more modern Mayo Hotel, shown here with a fleet of taxicabs ready for business, was completed in 1925.

enjoyed a swig of whiskey or two and a good poker game at times of his choosing.

Ruth Sheldon Knowles wrote: *He held himself aloof from the shoving, excited bargainers as though he were John D. Rockefeller. Inevitably, an eager seller would dare to stop him to offer a 40-acre undrilled lease. Sinclair, who had the campaign map in his head, would pause briefly, snap, "Wouldn't pay you a dime over fifty dollars an acre, but you can see me in the morning," and sweep on out toward the depot. On the train to Independence he would chuckle at the knowledge of what was happening in the lobby. He knew that the going price of acreage in the area of the offered lease was only $25 an acre and that, by his offer, he had effectively tied up under free option every acre anyone had to offer. When he returned to Tulsa the next day there would be a crowd of brokers waiting to sell him anything available.*

The Hotel Tulsa and the Exchange National Bank were soon too small for Sinclair. After buying and selling production companies for years, he huddled in New York City with leading financiers and attorneys, stitched together Sinclair Oil, and returned to Tulsa with the news. The next morning, April 22, 1916, the *Tulsa World's* lead story carried the headline:

Gigantic Oil Corporation Formed by Harry Sinclair
With $50,000,000 Capital
Will Be Fourth Largest in the Entire Country

Details of the deal weren't fully disclosed at the time. All told, 11 petroleum companies were joined to make Sinclair Oil.

The newspaper's J. A. M'Keever wrote: *The three refining companies which have gone into the new combination are Cudahy* (near Chicago), *Chanute and Milliken* (in Kansas and Oklahoma). *The physical properties of the new corporation to start with will have, at a very conservative calculation, a value of $55,000,000. The new company will be the* *largest strictly independent oil company in this country. Several hundred miles of pipe lines owned by the three refineries go into the deal. The Cudahy Company has 112 miles of pipeline, the Chanute refinery 128 miles and the Milliken Company 121 miles in Kansas and Oklahoma.* (Sinclair Oil would build a pipeline linking the Chicago refinery to oil in Oklahoma and Kansas.)

Sinclair said, "The combining of the producing, refining and marketing ends of the oil industry under one management gives the ideal method of playing the game. I want to deny the report that (Sinclair Oil) is organized to compete with Standard Oil Company. We expect to produce oil, to refine it and to sell it in markets of this country and the world in com-

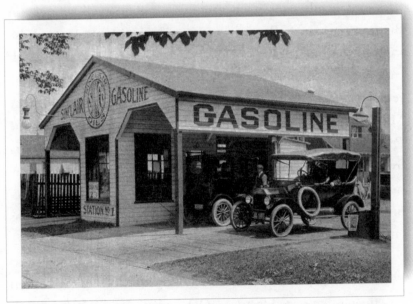

Gasoline was 23 cents a gallon when this photograph of a Sinclair filling station in New York was snapped in 1923, the year Harry Sinclair's horse Zev won the Kentucky Derby.

petition with anybody."

Only months before Sinclair Oil was founded, P. J. White, who had been partners with Sinclair since their oil activities at Independence, stepped aside – or was pushed. Either way, it was not surprising. Sinclair was meant to be at the helm, not share it.

Sinclair went on to build a new office building in Tulsa with the letter S carved in its roof line. He, his wife, Elizabeth, and their two children moved into a brick mansion in Tulsa. Their neighbors, all wealthy, included oil refiner Josh Cosden. In 1923, a long-odds horse named Zev won the Kentucky Derby with a time of 2:05, immediately followed by Martingale. Sinclair owned Zev; Cosden owned Martingale. The odds of this occurring, when all the factors are figured in, are off the charts.

A short time later, Cosden was broke. He had battled fires and windstorms while trying to run a small refinery in Bigheart (renamed Barnsdall), triumphed, and came to Tulsa shortly after the Cushing Field was discovered. A successful wild-catter and oil-field developer in his own right, he built a large refinery and Tulsa's first skyscraper, the million-dollar, 16-story Mid-Continent Building. Admirers began referring to Josh as the *Prince of Petroleum*. After spending princely sums on everything from his stunningly beautiful wife to racing stables and far away mansions, he went bust, made a comeback in Texas, but fell victim to the Great Depression. He died in 1940, his pockets as empty as a dry well.

The winner of the 1924 Kentucky Derby, incidentally, was Black Gold, owned by Tulsan Al Hoots' widow, Rosa, and named for "the oil that oozed from the Oklahoma soil." Sinclair was less earthy when picking a moniker for his steed. Zev was named for

Colonel J. W. Zevley, the millionaire oilman's attorney, whose services would come in handy.

After Zev raced to glory in '23, a scandal of national scope reared its ugly head regarding the no-bid leasing of Navy Department oil reserves in California and Wyoming. Mammoth Oil, a Sinclair company named for the vast quantities of crude it hoped to produce, was busily and expensively developing the Navy's Teapot Dome reserves in Wyoming.

Sinclair had obtained the lease from Interior Department Secretary Albert Fall, who came under suspicion of accepting separate bribes from Sinclair and Fred Doheny, a former mining prospector who was developing the California reserves. The issue pitted Democrats against Republicans, with the former pressing for a pound of flesh from Sinclair, Doheny, Fall and others, and the latter downplaying it as a "tempest in a teapot."

The scandal grew to symbolize corruption in government and took an incredible personal toll. President Warren Harding, who had approved the leases, died of a heart attack in August of 1923. Sinclair's faithful ally Connelly suffered a nervous breakdown years later while mopping up the mess at Teapot Dome. He blamed it on overwork and the energy-robbing altitude. Fall was convicted of accepting bribes, said to be in the six figures, and received a one-year sentence.

Sinclair and Doheny were charged with conspiring to defraud the federal government. Doheny was acquitted. Sinclair's first tribunal was declared a mistrial when the judge learned that he had employed detectives to track the jury. Ironically, the shadow work – perfectly legal – was done to ensure against jury-tampering.

Although Colonel Zevley testified that Sinclair had "loaned" Secretary Fall $25,000 in the summer of '23 and had not been repaid, a second jury acquitted Sinclair. But his troubles weren't over. He was convicted of contempt of the U.S. Senate and contempt of court – the first for refusing to answer one question, which he considered impertinent, from the political committee investigating the issue; the second for dogging the first jury with the private eyes. He had freely given more than 175,000 words of testimony to a variety of committees, but declined to testify at trial.

The scandal stretched across most of the 1920s, with appeals rising all the way to the Supreme Court. Sinclair served a six-month sentence in Washington, D.C., and was released in November of 1929 – angry and defiant.

"I was railroaded to jail in violation of common sense and common fairness," he stormed. "I cannot be contrite for sins which I know I have never committed."

Sinclair Oil lost an estimated $35 million in the Teapot Dome fiasco. It had envisioned producing up to 135 million barrels from the desolate, windswept place named for a rock that looked somewhat like a teapot. Instead, two million barrels were unearthed before the Wyoming lease was invalidated by a Supreme Court ruling in 1927. Worse, under terms of the lease agreement, Sinclair Oil paid the government up to 50 percent of its Teapot Dome oil sales and had built a $21 million pipeline from Wyoming to the Mid-Continent.

The dark curtain of the Great Depression was closing on the nation when Sinclair was free to return to his home and headquarters in New York. Like J. Paul Getty, he saw the terrible time as an opportunity, swooping up oil properties and companies for pennies on the dollar, including Richfield Oil of New York. In recognition of his skills and power, and in a sense saying *let bygones be bygones,* he was appointed under a Democratic administration to the Petroleum Industry War Council in 1942, a time when no-bid and often no-spec contracts were being awarded left and right. (Insight to the hell-for-leather war effort that frequently skipped the time-consuming bidding process: Dave Williams, of Williams Brothers of Tulsa, was instructed by Navy Admiral Ben Morrell to build a pipeline and fueling stations across the Isthmus of Panama. Seated across the desk from the admiral, Dave asked for the specifications. "There are none," Morrell replied. "We want to be able to pump any amount of crude oil in either direction across the isthmus at any time." The entire contracting process was completed in a matter of minutes.)

Sinclair skillfully ran and grew Sinclair Oil until his retirement in 1949, ending a remarkably long 33 years at the seat of power. On numerous occasions along the way, he established the price of Mid-Continent oil – something an independent producer from the Glenn Pool could only have dreamed of. He moved to Pasadena, California, served several more years on the Sinclair board, and died in 1956 at the age of 80.

Author Ruth Sheldon Knowles wrote that the news of his death surprised many: *He had become such a legend they thought he was already dead.*

(Atlantic merged with Richfield of California in 1966 to form Atlantic Richfield, or ARCO. Three years later, ARCO acquired Sinclair, adding 300,000 barrels a day to its crude-oil production. Sinclair today operates three refineries, two in Wyoming and a 60,000-barrel-per-day unit in Tulsa. Sinclair and its green dinosaur logo, which Harry Sinclair approved back in 1930, are still seen at service stations in 21 states.)

CLOSING THOUGHTS

THE BROAD, POWERFUL WAKE

t the crest of a gentle rise on U.S. 75 south of Glenpool's business corridor, Tulsa's skyline pops into view against the rolling prairie horizon. Just ahead, northwest of the traffic lights interrupting the continuous traffic flow on the four-lane ribbon of asphalt, is the birthplace for everything to be seen for miles and miles and miles.

The birthplace is the unmarked grave of the Ida Glenn No. 1. There, in the Glenn Pool, Oklahoma's first major oil field developed, well by well. There, too, the first natural gasoline plant west of the Mississippi came to life, birthing the state's natural gas processing industry. There, too, Oklahoma Natural Gas took its first big breaths. Because of the Glenn Pool, there were the major pipelines, the refineries, the banks, the expertise, the leaders, the workers, the hopes and the dreams.

Some have said that if the Glenn Pool hadn't been discovered by Bob Galbreath on that frosty morning a century ago, the great oil play and the development of an industry would have occurred sooner or later somewhere else. That's doubtlessly true, but it misses the point. It *was* Bob Galbreath, and it *was* the Glenn Pool.

Tulsa's impressive skyline, its schools and universities, its hospitals, parks, museums and cultural centers – these and much more are directly and forever connected to the man and the oil field. So, too, is Oklahoma's foremost business, its oil and gas industry.

Bob Blackburn, executive director of the Oklahoma Historical Society, says that the moment the Glenn Pool was born, "all of the capital and all of the trade" funneled into Tulsa. The city became the entrepreneur-friendly, unmatched mecca for financing, development and direction of the industry. For more than half a century, Tulsa was literally what it claimed to be, the *Oil Capital of the World.*

"As other oil came in, it flowed through the same circles," Blackburn explains. "So those oilmen attracted by the Glenn Pool would set up headquarters in Tulsa; they would send their landmen out to find other oil patches; they would finance the next drilling boom; they would provide the connection with the corporate interests in New York City, London, Amsterdam. The money had to come through a bank, and that was in Tulsa. It controlled the outflow of oil and the inflow of capital and men and material, and that laid the foundation for everything thereafter."

Oilmen, merchants and manufacturers continued to be drawn to Tulsa long after the Glenn Pool began to wane. They came to be a part – big or small – of the great game. In the process, they built a world-class city for the generations.

Cities are fortunate if they can lay claim to a few truly memorable leaders in their history. In the broad and powerful wake of the Glenn Pool, Tulsa attracted dozens. Many came with little more than ambition and optimism, but left gifts of lasting value, usefulness and beauty.

Bill Skelly broke into the oil industry as a $2.50-a-day tool dresser in Pennsylvania, eventually scraped enough money together for a drilling operation, and struck oil in Indiana. Four days later, his rig and his hopes went up in flames. Broke, the broad-shouldered oil-man rebuilt the rig himself, managing to coax the well back into production.

He arrived in Tulsa in 1912 – the same year the Cushing Field was discovered – had some luck in the Healdton and Hewitt fields of southern Oklahoma, and founded Skelly Oil in 1919. He seemed to have time for everything and everyone. Always neck-deep in building and promoting the city, he became known as *Mister Tulsa*, a born leader who drew no distinction between the elite and the common man – and was more comfortable

Bill Skelly

A Skelly fuel truck making deliveries in the 1920s.

with the latter.

For more than three decades, he headed up the greatest oil show on earth, the International Petroleum Exposition, which ran from 1923 to 1979. Designed as the industry's showcase, the IPE at its peak stretched for miles, drew hundreds of thousands of visitors, and displayed and demonstrated more than a billion dollars of equipment – at a single show.

In 1927, President Calvin Coolidge showed up to set off a simulated gusher. His appearance was followed six days later by a better-known name – the *Lone Eagle*, Charles Lindbergh, who arrived in his Spirit of St. Louis, the plane he had flown solo from New York to Paris that spring.

Cutting-edge oil technology was frequently developed in Oklahoma and displayed and demonstrated at the next Exposition. During the same show that featured Coolidge and Lindbergh, folks traveled to a field near Bixby to see how formations deep beneath the surface could be located by something called reflective seismography. John Karcher, a former Hennessey

Derricks pepper the evening sky at an early-year International Petroleum Exhibition. There was no show like it, which reinforced Tulsa's claim as The Oil Capital of the World.

farm boy with electrical engineering and physics degrees from the University of Oklahoma, was instrumental in developing the practical use of this technology. In December of 1928, the world's first well successfully drilled into a formation found by this technological wonder came to life near Seminole, scene of yet another Oklahoma oil boom. The industry had come a long way in a relatively short time since the dubious use of forked twigs, a mysterious black box called the Doodlebug, and a Texas boy with X-ray eyes were employed to find oil.

Crowd-pleasers at the Expositions ranged from the world's best oil-well firefighter – at the time, M. M. Kinley – to princess pageants and parades. At the 1930 event, attendees learned that Oklahoma oil during the previous five years had accounted for nearly one-third of the nation's production, 18 percent of the world's.

Demonstration wells were drilled at some of the shows; at

The International Petroleum Exhibition shown during the nation's bicentennial in 1976, three years before the IPE's 18th and final appearance.

one, a shooter triggered a light charge of nitroglycerin, the blast causing mud and water to drift onto the spectators.

Tulsa's Expo Center at the fairgrounds and its towering *Golden Driller* outside serve as reminders of the show. The Exposition, which operated without a dime of government help, formally closed shop in 1980. Tulsa no longer was the *Oil Capital of the World*. There were other cities, other shows, and other oil plays, including offshore. The IPE's executive directors, in a move reflective of oilmen's generosity throughout the history of Oklahoma, recommended that the Exposition's quarter-million in cash reserves be endowed equally to the University of Tulsa, the University of Oklahoma, and Oklahoma State University.

Early in the Great Depression, Bill Skelly made the bet of his lifetime regarding how long depressed oil prices would continue. To get his company through the tough times, he borrowed heavily from Standard Oil of New Jersey, but defaulted on the loan, giving it controlling interest in Skelly Oil.

The story took a weird twist in 1934 when Jersey Standard formed a holding company as a strategy against J. Paul Getty's continued pursuit of Tidewater Oil. Within this holding company, however, was not only the Tidewater stock, but the Skelly Oil stock as well. When Getty gained control of the holding company in 1937, he inadvertently acquired 57 percent of Skelly Oil, whose assets were valued at more than $56 million. It was like opening a box of Cracker Jacks and finding the prize of a lifetime.

Despite this series of events and the strikingly different personalities and backgrounds of the two oil giants, Bill Skelly continued to run and grow the company until three months before his death in 1957. Until then, few knew that Getty actually held the controlling interest. In World War II, J. Paul ran Skelly's Spartan Aircraft plant and the Spartan School of Aeronautics. During the war years, 16,000 pilots graduated from the school, which continues to turn out aviators today.

William Grove Skelly's legacy is broad and varied, ranging from the city's substantial aviation infrastructure to the University of Tulsa football stadium bearing his name. No one ever worked harder to champion Tulsa.

One of the most beautiful gifts ever bestowed on Tulsa or any other city came as an indirect result of the business-parting of two bullheaded brothers.

Although Waite Phillips loved his older brother Frank, the two often butted heads, causing them to part in 1914. Frank stayed and built Phillips Petroleum in Bartlesville; Waite moved south to Okmulgee. As Waite's son, Elliott, explained much later: "If two men are riding the same trail, one has to be in front." *(Beyond the Hills, The Journey of Waite Phillips,* by Michael Wallis.)

Waite struck oil just south of Okmulgee in 1915, built an integrated oil company, and moved to Tulsa in 1918. He and his wife, Genevieve, built Villa Philbrook in the late twenties. The home's interior featured the world's finest marble and handcrafted woods; its exterior glistened from the ground marble mixed with the stucco. After residing there in splendor for fewer than 12 years, they moved into the Mayo Hotel and made a gift of the Italian-renaissance mansion and its 23-acre gardens. There, the Philbrook Museum of Art opened in 1939.

At one time, Waite's land holdings exceeded 700,000

Waite Phillips

Frank Phillips

acres. In 1942, he gave a 127,000-acre ranch in New Mexico to the Boy Scouts of America. The first Scouts to arrive there paid a buck-twenty-five for a unique week in one of the most beautiful parts of the West. Phillips' Beacon and Philtower buildings, gems of downtown Tulsa, were given to endow the museum and Scout ranch, respectively. More than six million people have toured Philbrook. It and the Gilcrease Museum across town are considered to be among the best in the nation.

Described as private and reserved, at times appearing aloof, Waite understood giving. He knew that a poor person giving his coat to keep another warm was no less generous – perhaps more so – than a multimillionaire donating a mansion and a ranch.

In many cases, the Glenn Pool's wake is hidden in plain sight. When the Philbrook Museum underwent a massive expansion in the early 1990s, it was seamlessly handled by Flintco, a family-owned descendant of Tulsa Rig, Reel & Manufacturing. In 1908, opportunities in the Glenn Pool lured Charles Flint from his home in Vermont to Tulsa, where he partnered in the business of providing wooden derricks and related equipment. Gaining controlling interest in the venture in 1914, Flint established lumberyards in towns that emerged as the oil boom migrated through Oklahoma. The business transformed into construction, which in turn led to general contracting in 1936.

Adopted in 1972, the Flintco name is associated with downtown Tulsa's tallest building, the beautiful topping of its first skyscraper, its Performing Arts Center, and the University of Tulsa's Reynolds Center. In Oklahoma City, there are the Myriad Convention Center, Ford Center, Cox Convention Center,

National Cowboy & Western Heritage Museum, Civic Center Music Hall, Sam Noble Museum of Natural History, and the recent state Capitol dome. These structures and numerous others are linked to Charles Flint's success in the Glenn Pool.

"The business grew with the oil business," says Robin Flint Ballenger, chairman of Flintco's board of directors and the granddaughter of founder Charles Flint.

In 1924, Joe LaFortune's third and newest job in Tulsa consisted of answering the phone and writing a four-page newsletter, *The Natural Gasser.* After growing tired of explaining to callers that his boss, W. K. Warren, was strictly in the business of buying and selling natural gasoline, he added the words *Just Natural Gasoline* to the bottom of the newsletter cover.

Some 31 years later in 1955, the Indiana native was the second-largest stockholder of Warren Petroleum when it was sold to Gulf Oil. The sale price broke the record established in Tulsa when a couple of ranchers, who got their start in the Glenn Pool, sold McMan Oil almost four decades earlier.

LaFortune and Warren individually donated millions to the betterment of Tulsa.

Joe LaFortune

W. K. Warren

Their most readily apparent gifts are LaFortune Park, with its golf courses, tennis courts, baseball diamond and swimming pool, and, just up the hill, Saint Francis Hospital, created by the Warren Foundation. (Joe LaFortune also provided a different sort of legacy. His son Bob served as mayor when downtown underwent a $158 million revitalization program in the 1970s, spearheaded by The Williams Companies. Today, Bob LaFortune's nephew Bill is the city mayor. Like his uncle before him, he is leading a sweeping revitalization program, called Vision 2025.)

Literally dozens have followed in the philanthropic footsteps of these men and those who preceded them. Sixteen of the top 25 philanthropic organizations in Oklahoma are rooted in oil.

The Glenn Pool is to oil "what a kickoff is to a football game," says Jenkin Lloyd Jones Jr., the grandson of the newspaperman who bought *The Tulsa Tribune* from Charles Page in 1919.

The perception persists, however, that the game surely must be over. This was expressed as far back as the early 1920s when Tulsa attorney Earl Sneed conceived the idea for the International Petroleum Exposition. The perception was untrue then and remains inaccurate today.

Larry Claxton, Oklahoma Corporation Commission's manager of statistics, points out that nearly 50,000 men and women are "directly involved" in the state's oil and gas industry, which affects the jobs of tens of thousands of others. Oklahoma's oil and gas industry accounted for $11 billion in revenues in 2004.

"It is still a very viable industry," Claxton says, noting that

Oklahoma is the number-two producer of natural gas and the number-six oil producer in the nation. He adds that 85 percent of the production is handled by small independents. In some cases, it amounts to a lone operator checking on a handful of wells on his or her way home from town or a day on the farm.

Oil and gas continue to be important players in Tulsa's economy. Not including marketers or distributors, more than 540 companies directly involved in oil and gas operate in or near the city, including 148 exploration and development firms, 132 producers, 55 field-services outfits, 58 equipment dealers, and 39 supply houses.

State, regional and worldwide scientific and trade associations continue to base their operations in Tulsa. The largest is the American Association of Petroleum Geologists, organized in Tulsa in 1917 and currently serving 31,000 members in 118 nations. Others include the Society for Exploration Geophysicists, with 20,000 members in more than 100 countries; the Petroleum Equipment Institute, representing 1,643 companies in 82 countries; the Gas Processors Association, representing 90 percent of the nation's production of gas liquids; the Gas Processors Suppliers Association; and the International Society of Energy Advocates. As noted previously, the *Oil & Gas Journal,* circulated worldwide, continues to be published in Tulsa.

In terms of revenue generated and wells drilled, natural gas – once considered a nuisance – overtook oil in Oklahoma in the early 1990s. In 2004, more than 1,800 new gas wells were drilled in the state, compared with fewer than 400 oil wells. Claxton notes that most of the state's oil happens to be sandwiched between its two major gas fields, the Arkoma Basin in the southeast and the more mature Anadarko Basin in the northwest.

The public's image and knowledge of the oil and gas industry have long been less than ideal. But thanks in part to an idea conceived in the 1980s by independent oilman Harlan Krumme, of Bristow, it is improving in Oklahoma. Krumme and fellow Oklahoma oilmen envisioned a nationwide education program, but it failed to gain federal traction in Washington.

"Rather than giving up, the group returned to Oklahoma determined to show them that it would work here," says Mike Terry, executive director of the Oklahoma Energy Resources Board.

Phillips Petroleum, now ConocoPhillips, and other major oil companies agreed to support the effort if it included environmental clean-up of abandoned oil and gas sites. Since 1993, when the OERB was organized, the nationally unparalleled program has restored 6,000-plus orphaned or abandoned sites and helped teachers educate more than 500,000 school children about the oil and gas industry in Oklahoma.

Funding for the OERB's sweeping educational and environmental programs comes from the state's oil and natural gas producers and royalty owners, who contribute one-tenth of one percent of their wellhead revenues. They are asked each year if they agree with how the OERB has spent their money; if they don't, their portion is returned – with interest.

Today's oil and gas activities may seem a long mental and physical journey from the Glenn Pool, but Terry and others believe that modern-day Oklahoma and the Glenn Pool are intrinsically connected.

Referring to the human energy and spirit that created –

and continues to create – wealth from the ground, Terry says:
"The Glenn Pool is *who* we are."

NOTES AND CREDITS

The Glenn Pool has been historically referred to as the greatest oil field in the world during its period of dominance, which is generally considered from 1907 to 1912, when the Cushing Field to its west began its rapid development. In recognition of the enormous Baku oil fields of Russia, the author has chosen to describe the Glenn Pool as the greatest oil field in America. The author notes here, however, that it could be argued that the Glenn Pool *was* the greatest *single* oil field in the world during the 1907-1912 time period, when measured collectively by these terms: production volume, crude-oil quality, and development of the industry infrastructure. Oklahoma Geological Survey production figures for the Glenn Pool from 1907 through 1914 are: 1907, 19,927,300 barrels; 1908, 20,494,313; 1909, 18,946,740; 1910, 19,236,914; 1911, 13,880,118; 1912, 10,495,518; 1913, 9,469,870; and 1914, 8,677,589.

Quotations from people interviewed for this book are used in the present tense. For example, in a scene that depicts the drilling of the Ida Glenn No. 1, a living oilman provides his perspective regarding the arduous process involved on a cable-tool rig. His voice is in the present tense. In that same segment, two of the rig's original crew members are quoted from the century-old event. Their voices are in the past tense. The author employed this method to differentiate between the two time periods – then and now – and to provide a sense of currency as well.

Numerous sources were used, often collectively, by the author to portray scenes, to reach conclusions, and to provide perspective regarding not only the Glenn Pool but the oil industry and life in Oklahoma and the United States. Specific sources used verbatim in this book are cited and credited within the affected segment of the text.

We express deep appreciation for the following resources, which made this book possible.

A Fool's Enterprise, The Life of Charles Page, Opal Bennefield Clark
A History of the International Petroleum Exposition and Congress, James P. Walker
American Association of Petroleum Geologists, the foundation's Energy Resources Library, paper by Edgar Wesley Owen
An Adventure Called Skelly, Roberta Ironside
Beyond the Hills, The Journey of Waite Phillips, Michael Wallis
Birth of Guthrie: Oklahoma's Run of 1889 and Life in Guthrie in 1889 and the 1890's, Lloyd H. McGuire Jr.
Bloodland: A True Story of Oil, Greed and Murder on the Osage, Dennis McAuliff
Discovering Oil Again, Oklahoma Energy Centennial, Bartlesville Examiner-Enterprise
Early Oklahoma Oil: A Photographic History, Kenny Franks
Energy — 75 Years After Glenn Pool, Metropolitan Chamber of Commerce, Tulsa Magazine, Bob Gregory
Genesis of Oklahoma Oil Banking, Paul F. McGuire
Ghost Towns of Oklahoma, John W. Morris
Glenn Pool ... and a little oil town of yesteryear, Frank Galbreath

Glenpool Public Schools

Glenn Pool Field – U.S.A., a geological paper, Michael D. Kuykendall and Thomas E. Matson

Harlow's Weekly

History of the Glennpool Oil Field, a master's thesis, J. Vere Frazier Jr., University of Oklahoma

Riot and Remembrance: The Tulsa Race War and Its Legacy, James S. Hirsch

Joplin Globe

Kiefer City Hall

King of the Wildcatters – The Life and Times of Tom Slick, Ray Miles

McFarlin Library, University of Tulsa

Mid-Continent Oil and Gas Association of Oklahoma

Mounds Enterprise

Mounds Historical Society

Oil & Gas Journal

Oil in Oklahoma, Robert Gregory

Oil Investors' Journal

Oil Man: The Story of Frank Phillips, Michael Wallis

Oil! Titan of the Southwest, Carl Rister

Oklahoma Corporation Commission

Oklahoma Geological Survey, Oklahoma Oil: Past, Present and Future, Dan T. Boyd

Oklahoma, Land of the Fair God, Odie Faulk

Oklahoma: The Land and Its People, Kenny Franks and Paul F. Lambert

Pawhuska Capital-Journal

Phillips: The First 66 Years, Phillips Petroleum Company

Sapulpa Herald

Sapulpa Historical Society

Sapulpa Public Library

Sapulpa Light

Snapshots in Time, A collection of little stories about one of America's great companies, Doug Hicks

Spindletop, James A. Clark and Michel T. Halbouty

The Dicky Bird Was Singing, Bob Duncan

The Gentleman, The Life of Joseph A. LaFortune, Odie B. Faulk, James H. Thomas, Carl N. Tyson

The Greatest Gamblers, Ruth Sheldon Knowles

The History of Tulsa, Oklahoma, a City With a Personality, Clarence Douglas

The Inflation Calculator, S. Morgan Friedman

The McMan, The Lives of Robert M. McFarlin and James A. Chapman, Carl Tyson, James Thomas, Odie Faulk.

The Oil Business as I Saw it, a Half Century with Sinclair, W. L. Connelly

The Oklahoma Oil Industry, Kenny Franks

The Prize: The Epic Quest for Oil, Money and Power, Daniel Yergin

The Rush Begins, Kenny Franks

The Tulsa Tribune

The 89ers: Oklahoma Land Rush, Kathlyn Baldwin

Thomas Gilcrease and His National Treasure, introduction, Fred A. Myers

Tulsa! Biography of the American City, Danney Goble

Tulsa City-County Libraries, Biography Resources Center

Tulsa Democrat

Tulsa Genealogical Society Library

Tulsa Historical Society

Tulsa's Magic Roots, Nina Lane Dunn

Tulsa, Oil Capital of the World, James O. Kemm

Tulsa, Oklahoma: A City with a Personality, Clarence B. Douglas

Tulsa Preservation Commission

Tulsa World

Tune of the Hickory Stick, 75 Years in the Jenks Public Schools, Joyce Elliott Nichols

Voices from the Oil Fields, Kenny Franks

Special thanks to the following for photographic contributions:

David Sheffel

Sapulpa Historical Society

University of Tulsa McFarlin Library - Special Collections

Bartlesville Area History Museum

Tulsa Historical Society

The Beryl Ford Collection

The Rockefeller Archive Center

Gulf Oil Corporation

Oil Weekly

Oklahoma Heritage Association

Tulsa County Historical Society — Daisy Johnson Collection

University of Oklahoma Library — Western History Collection

The Harry Shobe Family

Sand Springs Museum

Tulsa City-County Libraries Archives

Warren Foundation

Chapman Trust

James O. Kemm Collection

Don Sibley, Tulsa Metro Chamber

CONTRIBUTORS

Sharon Baldwin

Bob Blackburn

Carol Campbell

Watermelon Campbell

Opal Bennefield Clark

Larry Claxton

Rick Erickson

Becky Frank

Jack Frank

Kenny Franks

Steve Geddie

Jim Gipson

Ruth Ellen Henry

Stan Hicks

Jenkin Lloyd Jones Jr.

Jim Kemm

John Laird

Bob LaFortune

Don Lightner

Tom Matson

Ken Neal

Eddie Rongey

Ira Rongey

Chuck Schnake

Alva Shanks

Sam Shanks

Pearl Sharpe

Danny Sherrer

Harry Shobe

Rita Stover

Mike Terry

Michelle Thomas

Steve Turnbo

Doris R. Yocham

BEHIND THE BOOK

A favorable newspaper review of a Glenpool restaurant led to the writing of this book and the production of a 30-minute video documentary.

Chuck Schnake, chairman emeritus of the Tulsa public-relations firm of Schnake Turnbo Frank, and his wife, Carol, had finished eating at Mamadou's Restaurant and were driving home on U.S. 75 when he noticed a historical marker about the Glenn Pool. He recalled being at the unveiling of the marker back in 1972 and realized that the great oil field was nearing its one-hundredth birthday.

"I really didn't know much about the Glenn Pool," he says, explaining that he began researching its history. "The more I read, the more interested I became. I kept thinking, *There ought to be something more than that little marker.*"

Following a creative session at Schnake Turnbo Frank,

Explorer Pipeline agreed to supply the substantial "seed money" necessary for the book, the video, and related projects. (One of Explorer's vast tank farms and numerous pump stations is on the outskirts of Glenpool. The company's 28-inch refined-petroleum pipeline originates in Lake Charles, Louisiana, swings over to Port Arthur, Texas, and comes up through Glenpool, where it reduces to 24 inches in diameter and continues on to Hammond, Indiana, near Chicago. Headquartered in Tulsa, Explorer is owned by CITGO, ChevronTexaco, ConocoPhillips, Shell, Sunoco, and Marathon. More than 600,000 barrels of refined products are transported in the pipeline around the clock.)

"Taking part in the Glenn Pool centennial projects has served as another opportunity for our company to give back to the community," says Tim Felt, president of Explorer Pipeline. "The Glenn Pool put Oklahoma on the map. The state could have looked a lot different without it."

The documentary video was produced by Jack Frank Productions, of Tulsa. At the time *Nearly Forgotten* went to press, key sponsors of the book, the video and related projects included: ConocoPhillips, the Oklahoma Energy Resources Board, The Bank of Oklahoma Foundation, The Grace and Franklin Bernsen Foundation, The Anne and Henry Zarrow Foundation, Chesapeake Energy Corporation and Magellan Midstream Partners, as well as Explorer.

The non-profit Glenn Pool Centennial Commission was formed to steer and boost the efforts. Information about the Commission's activities can be found at www.glenpoolcentennial.com.

INDEX

Mounds Enterprise 30, 60-61, 63, 65, 149
Mounds Historical Society 55, 149
Mounds, Oklahoma 24, 26, 30, 54-55, 60-61, 63-66,
68-69, 72, 81, 84, 149
Muskogee Weekly Phoenix 20
Muskogee, Oklahoma 20, 56, 58, 66-68, 118
Myers, Olivia 53
Myriad Convention Center 141

National Bank of Tulsa 124
National Cowboy & Western Heritage Museum 142
National Oil and Development 85
National Supply Company 65
Navy Department Oil Reserves 129
Neodesha, Kansas 24
Nevada Berryhill 64
New Mexico 141
New York 32, 43, 59, 126, 130, 134, 136
New York and British financiers 80
New York Oil 85

Ohio 9, 11, 43
Oil & Gas Journal 93, 106, 144, 149
Oil Capital of the World 19, 84, 90, 92, 99, 134, 137-
138, 151
Oil Investors' Journal 65, 80, 84, 86, 88, 93, 149
Oil Well Supply Company 65
Oklahoma 37, 44-45, 53, 87, 90, 104, 106, 110, 124,
126-127, 136

Rogers, Bill 58

Rogers, Harry 85, 106

Rogers, Will 37, 59, 91

Roller, "Two-Gun" Ike 84

Rongey, Eddie 1, 3, 4, 102, 153

Rongey, Ira 28, 153

Roosevelt, President Theodore 23, 87, 91

Sac and Fox Indian Agency 16

Saint Francis Hospital 143

Saint Mary's Hall 108

Saint Simeon's Episcopal Home 107

Salvation Army 110-111

Sam Noble Museum of Natural History 142

San Antonio, Texas 69, 108

Sand Springs Children's Home 111, 113, 114-117, 120

Sand Springs Museum 117, 151

Sand Springs Railway 112

Sand Springs, Oklahoma 110-113, 115-117, 120

Santa Fe 58

Sapulpa Historical Society 53, 93, 150-151

Sapulpa Light 64, 150

Sapulpa Oil Refinery 94

Sapulpa, Oklahoma 22, 53, 54, 56, 58, 64-67, 72, 83-84, 90-95, 123, 150

Savoy Oil 85

Selby Oil 85

Selby, F. M. 83

Seminole, Oklahoma 137